Introduction

"architecture and landscape combined harmoniously ..."
From the statement of Outstanding Universal Value, UNESCO, for Bath World Heritage Site

This book tells the story of the creation of Georgian Bath. We hope that it will give you an insight into the splendid architecture of this city, which was declared a World Heritage Site by UNESCO in 1987.

Bath is an architectural masterpiece, one of Europe's most beautiful and elegant cities. We hope to show, however, that Georgian Bath was not just built as a work of art. The search for profit and the moods of fashion mattered as much to people in the 18th century as they do to us today. The building of Georgian Bath was a result of one of those moments in history which are impossible to plan for, moments when individual self interest and the interests of the community, idealism and commerce, architecture and taste, love and money all point in the same direction.

Many of the images in this book are drawn from the Building of Bath Collection, housed and open to the public at the Countess of Huntingdon's Chapel. This building was constructed in 1765 and was rescued from decay and restored by the Bath Preservation Trust in 1984.

The Bath Preservatio
to protect Bath's spe
of the encircling landscape. In the 1970s it was largely the influence of the Trust which halted the tide of reckless development that had swept away over a thousand historic buildings in only a few years.

The Trust has also restored No. 1 Royal Crescent and furnished it as it might have looked in the late 18th century. This Georgian Townhouse, a few minutes walk away, is also open to the public. To see across Bath's splendid landscape setting you can also visit Beckford's Tower, the retreat of one of Georgian England's wealthiest and most colourful personalities.

We hope that an insight into the city's historic architecture makes Bath a more rewarding place for visitors and residents alike.

Edward Bayntun-Coward
Chairman of Bath Preservation Trust

www.bath-preservation-trust.org.uk
www.bptlearning.org.uk

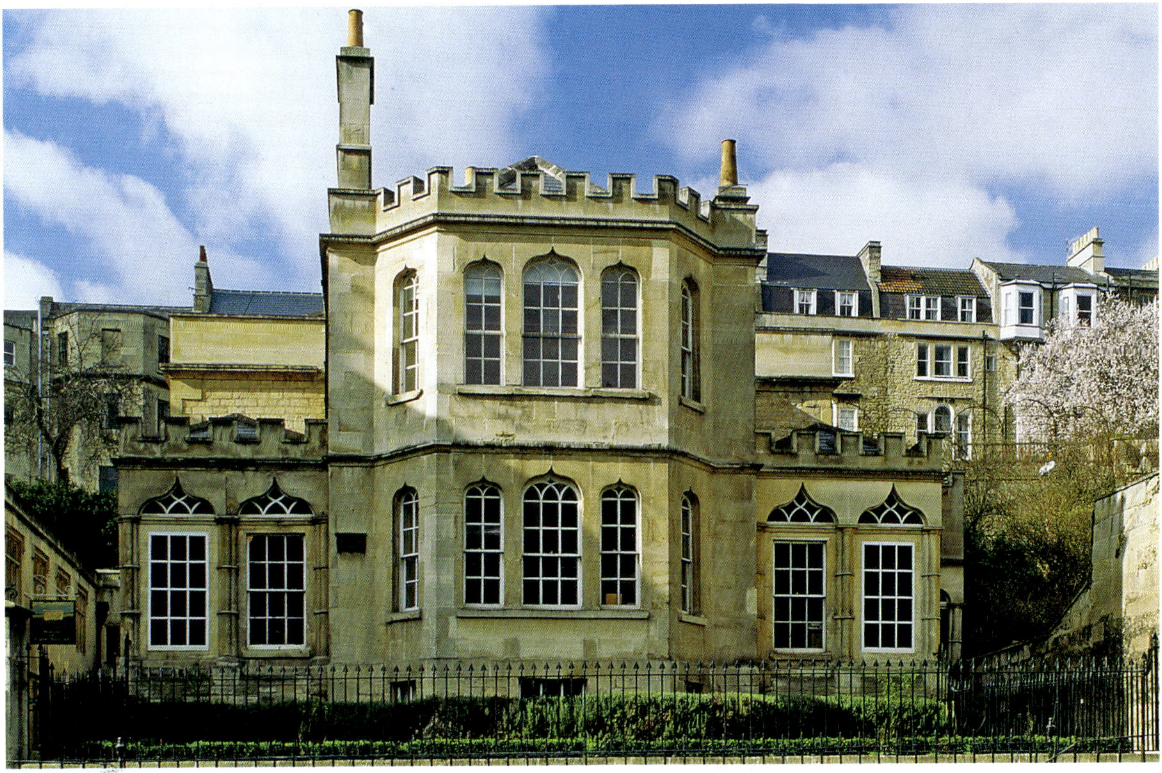

Fig. 1 The Countess of Huntingdon's Chapel, Bath

PRE-GEORGIAN BATH

Bath exists because of its hot springs. Legend has it that in ancient times Prince Bladud *(Fig.1)*, the son of a British King - and the father of King Lear - was afflicted by leprosy and left the royal court to become a wandering swineherd. His pigs contracted leprosy too. One day they were rooting for acorns in the mud near the springs and emerged with their hides miraculously cleansed. Bladud waded in himself and was also cured of his disease.

Whatever the truth of this tale, the springs were a sacred shrine in Celtic times. It was the Romans, however, who built the first baths in the 1st century AD; excavations have shown what a magnificent religious centre their "Aquae Sulis" was. But when the Romans retreated from Britain in the 5th century the stone baths and temples fell into neglect and in 577 AD the deserted city was sacked by the Saxon warlords.

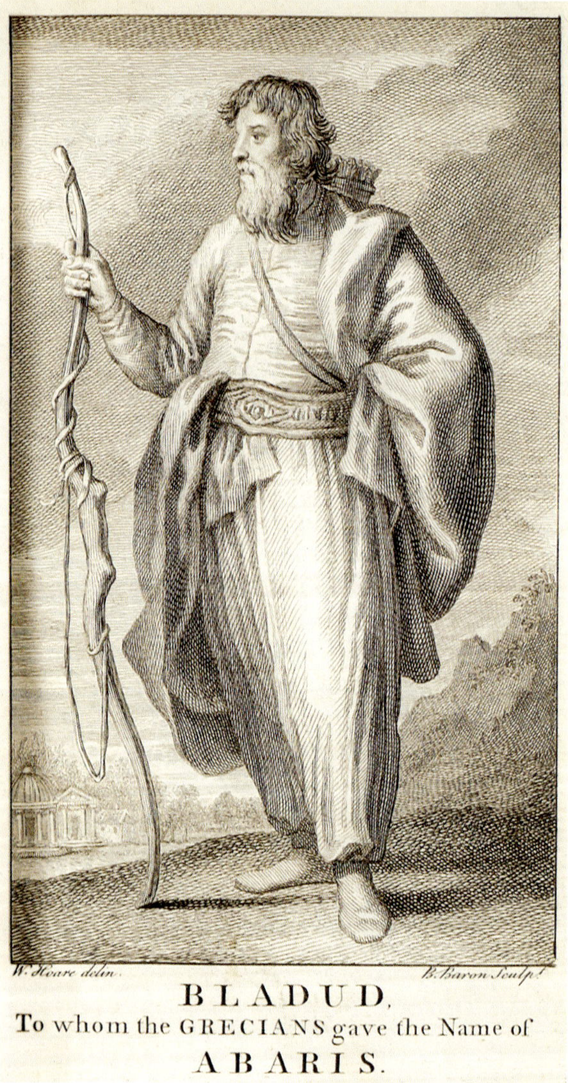

A poem of the time lamented: "*Wondrous is this masonry, shattered by the fates. The city has been broken and the fortifications raised by giants are crumbling. The roofs have fallen and the towers are in ruins...*" A renowned monastery, built with Roman masonry, was founded within the Roman precinct and in 973 AD King Edgar, so-called "first King of all England", was crowned here. This wealthy religious establishment, together with the wool trade, brought prosperity to Saxon and medieval Bath.

The "King's Bath" - the renovated Roman reservoir - was already in medical use in Norman times but widespread interest in the hot springs did not revive until the 16th century when people afflicted by leprosy, small pox, infertility or other ailments flocked to Bath to seek cures by swimming in the "miraculous" waters. After Charles II's visit in 1663 pumps were installed to encourage visitors to drink the waters.

The famous map of Bath on the facing page was drawn by Joseph Gilmore, a Bristol mathematician, in 1694 *(Fig. 2)*. The margin of this map depicts in detail the city's baths, churches and many fine lodging houses. These were built by enterprising local men eager to profit from the growing numbers of visitors to the baths. The broad windows and flamboyant stone ornaments you can see on these buildings advertised convenience and comfort.

But 17th century Bath, though pretty, still had an unsophisticated rural air. Most houses were much humbler and plainer than the lodging houses illustrated by Gilmore. Water ran in open gutters down the dirty, unlit streets. A battlemented medieval wall still surrounded the city.

A hundred years later Gilmore's city had disappeared and "Georgian Bath" had taken its place. The walls were pulled down, the surrounding farmland built over and nearly every building Gilmore had drawn demolished. Why was Bath transformed so suddenly and so completely?

Fig.1 Prince Bladud, by William Hoare
from John Wood's "Essay towards a description of Bath", 1749

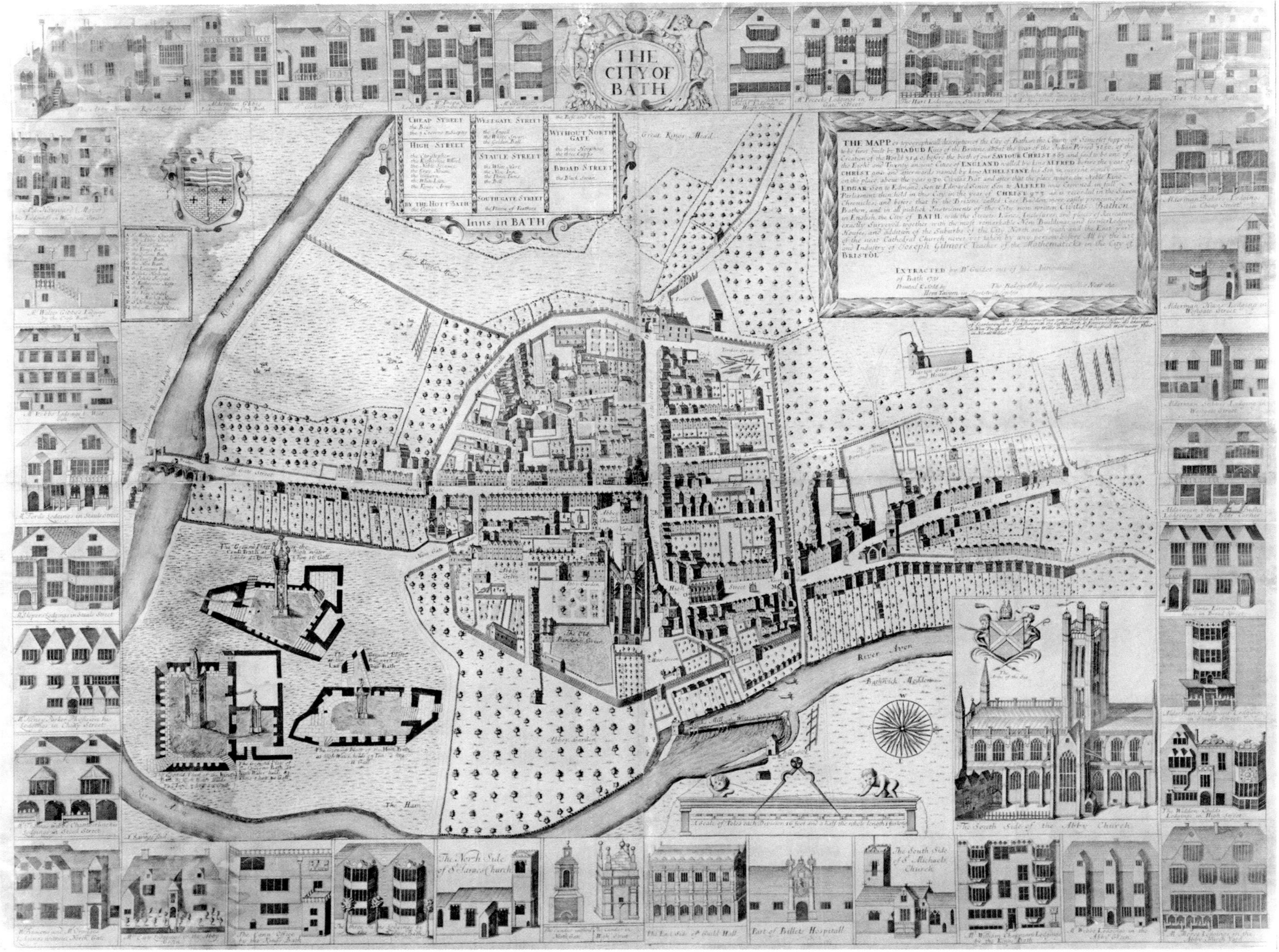

Fig.2 ***"The City of Bath"*** *by Joseph Gilmore, 1694*

Bath "Valley Of Pleasure"

Queen Anne's celebrated visits to the baths in 1702 and 1703 gave Bath the seal of Royal approval and the fashionable elite of the Court followed in her wake. Accustomed to spending much of the year amusing themselves in London they now came to Bath for a season, to take the waters, enjoy each others' company and gamble in a new setting.

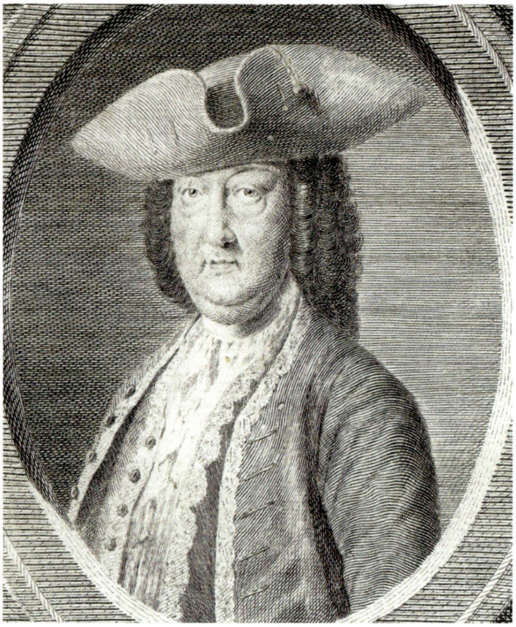

Fig.1 Richard "Beau" Nash
from Oliver Goldsmith's "Life of Richard Nash", 1762

Bath's sudden popularity with fashionable society might have faded, however, had it not been for the arrival in 1704 of a penniless adventurer named Richard Nash *(Fig. 1)*. "Beau" Nash was a professional gambler with a notorious past who saw that the spa resort needed to be more sophisticated and entertaining if it was to remain in fashion.

In 1705 Nash was appointed Master of Ceremonies, his predecessor having been killed in a duel. In this new role he introduced higher standards of polite behaviour and encouraged the provision of better facilities for visitors. Streets were lit and cleaned, promenades laid out and an Assembly Room and a Pump Room built. Duelling was banned, gambling was organised and rowdy old provincial customs such as cock-fighting or bull-baiting were banished from the sight of polite society.

By 1734, the date of this view *(Fig.2)*, Bath was still a small, walled city but no longer was it a resort catering solely for the sick. Due to these improvements it had acquired a reputation as a seasonal resort for the gentry and nobility, and fine new houses were being built for them to stay in.

How did visitors spend their time in this "valley of pleasure"? As a new arrival you might buy a "Bath Guide" *(Fig.3)* to find out about rules of etiquette, places to visit and the shops, churches and baths. You could begin the day with an early morning visit to the baths for your health followed by a glass of the mineral water in the Pump Room. There might be a Public Breakfast, accompanied by music, and the rest of the day could be spent in the coffee houses and luxurious shops and in strolling along the promenades or making excursions into the surrounding countryside. For the evening you could buy tickets to the theatre or one of the rival Assembly Rooms. Costing £20,000 to build, the New Assembly Rooms *(Fig. 4)* opened in 1771 and contained magnificent rooms for balls, cards, tea and concerts.

The greatest delight Bath offered, however, was the pleasure of the fellow company - the chance to strike up new friendships, to flirt, to find an aristocratic husband or a wealthy wife, to flaunt new clothes, to frequent the coffee rooms and bookshops and complain about the extortionate prices....

Almost every famous figure of the 18th century visited Bath at one time or another. It was Britain's leading resort throughout the period but its clientele became less exclusive as the city grew in size and popularity. By the end of the century there were nearly 500 lodging houses and a resident population of 33,000, making Bath one of the most populous cities in Britain.

After 1800, however, the seasonal visitors began to drift away to the seaside resorts of Brighton or Weymouth or the spa at Cheltenham. Victorian Bath became a pleasant place to pass a respectable retirement, a sedate city of military officers and naval men, clergy, widows and the occasional literary luminary. They had less money to spend on "improvements" to the historic city than their Georgian predecessors and, as a result, left the 20th century an unspoilt, if dilapidated, legacy of fine buildings.

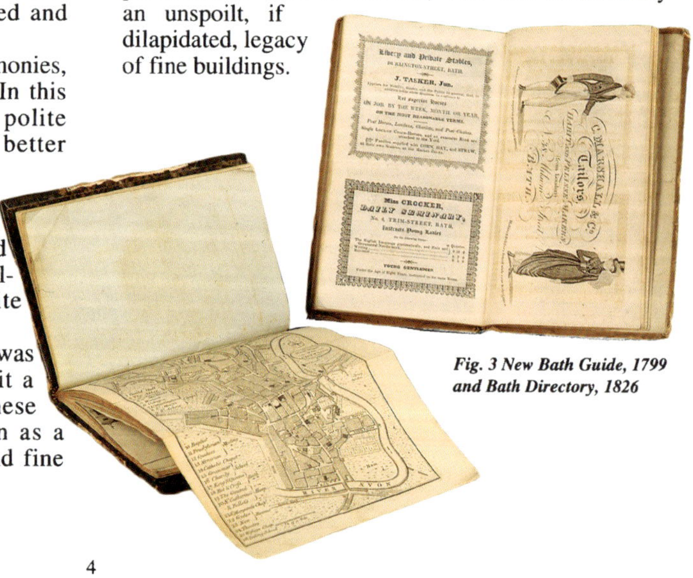

Fig. 3 New Bath Guide, 1799 and Bath Directory, 1826

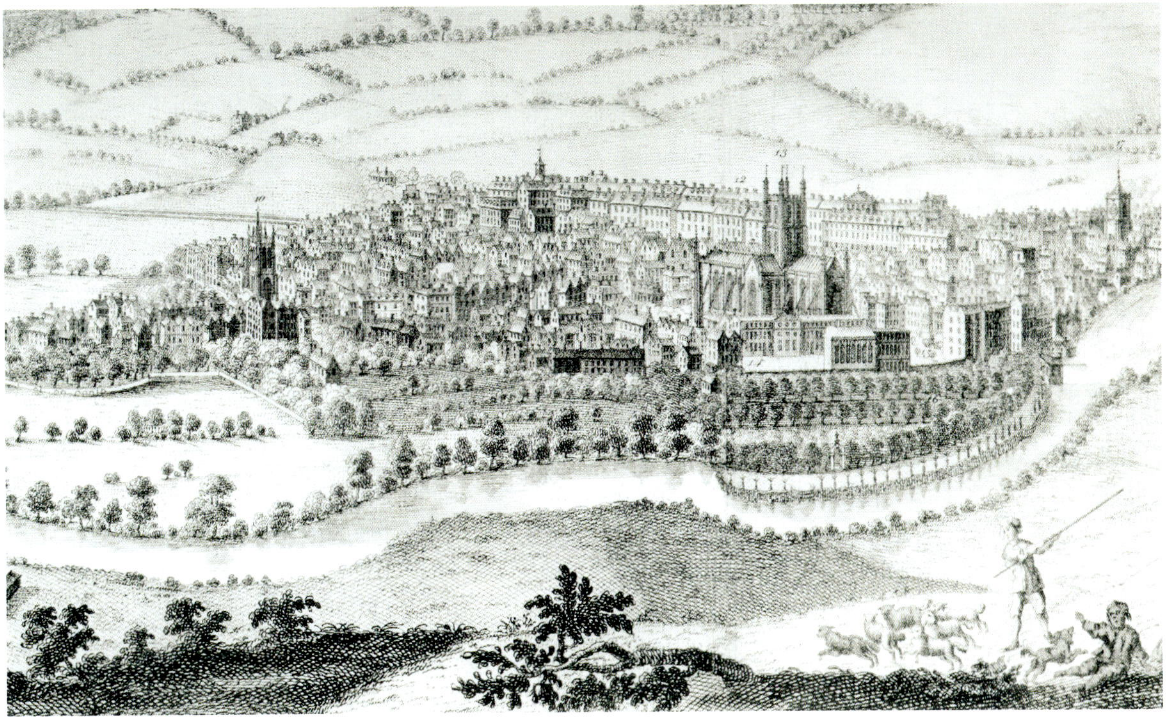

Fig.2 Detail from "A South East Prospect of Bath"
Engraving by Samuel and Nathaniel Buck, 1734

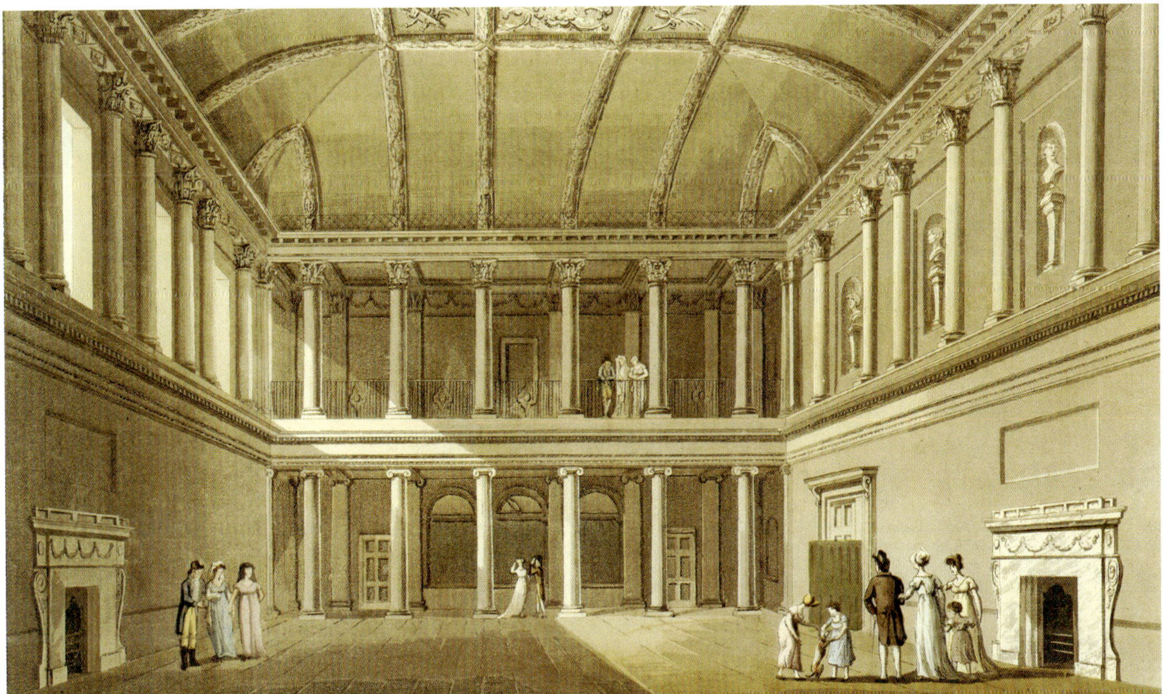

Fig. 4 The Concert Room at the New Assembly Rooms
by J C Nattes, 1805

John Wood and Town Planning

Bath's architectural splendour is inevitably associated with the name of John Wood (1704 - 54), the architect and developer who established the city's architectural style and whose fine new buildings were one of its greatest attractions.

John Wood was the son of a humble Bath builder. He was apprenticed as a carpenter and whilst still a youth travelled to London and Yorkshire to acquire architectural experience.

Queen Square (1729 - 39) *Fig.1*
Wood returned to his native Bath in 1727 with ambitious plans to restore the city to its Roman magnificence. His first successful development, Queen Square, was as grand as any of the new squares he had seen in London. The square's shape was admirably suited to the lifestyle of Bath because the houses enclosed an attractive space in which the visiting company might assemble and promenade in. On the north side it was overlooked by an imposing facade which appeared to belong to a splendid palace but which, in fact, concealed seven more modest houses. This was the first time in Britain that a terrace of individual houses was successfully unified behind a "palace front".

The King's Circus (1754 - 67) *Fig. 2*
Wood died the year he began The King's Circus and the thirty houses were completed to his design by his son John Wood the Younger (1727 - 81) who was also an architect and developer. The Circus was originally paved over - the clump of towering plane trees you can see there today was planted several decades later - and Wood proposed a statue of King George II on horseback, never erected, for the centre.

The Circus was Britain's first circular street. What inspired this novel design? The Colosseum in Rome - which has tiers of columns on the outside - was an obvious source and one contemporary did indeed describe The Circus as "the Colosseum turned outside-in". Wood was an admirer of the architecture of the classical world and particularly proud of Bath's historical link with Rome but he was also passionately loyal to the city's British inheritance and he intended The Circus to stand as a link with the city's mystical history.

An obsessive archaeologist, he believed that, long before the Romans ever came to Britain, Prince Bladud had built for his Druid priests a circular temple similar to Stonehenge near the site of the Circus. Indeed, the Circus shares the same diameter as Stonehenge - according to Wood's rather distorted measurements - and the stone acorns running round its parapet were a reminder of the legend of how Prince Bladud discovered the hot springs.

Royal Crescent (1767 - 74) *Fig. 3*
Queen Square and The Circus formed enclosed spaces but John Wood the Younger's Royal Crescent was laid out to embrace the open landscape. This change of view reflected the growing appreciation of the unspoilt beauty of Nature, a taste we call the "Picturesque".

It was the first crescent in Britain - what inspired this unique shape? It is possible that Wood the Younger inherited his father's theory that a crescent-shaped Druid "Temple of the Moon" once stood near to Stonehenge; or, alternatively, he may have intended the shape to reflect the curving contours of the landscape. It is also true that one third of The Circus stood by itself for seven years until the money to complete the development was found - could the sight of this single segment standing alone in the landscape have given John Wood the Younger the idea for a crescent?

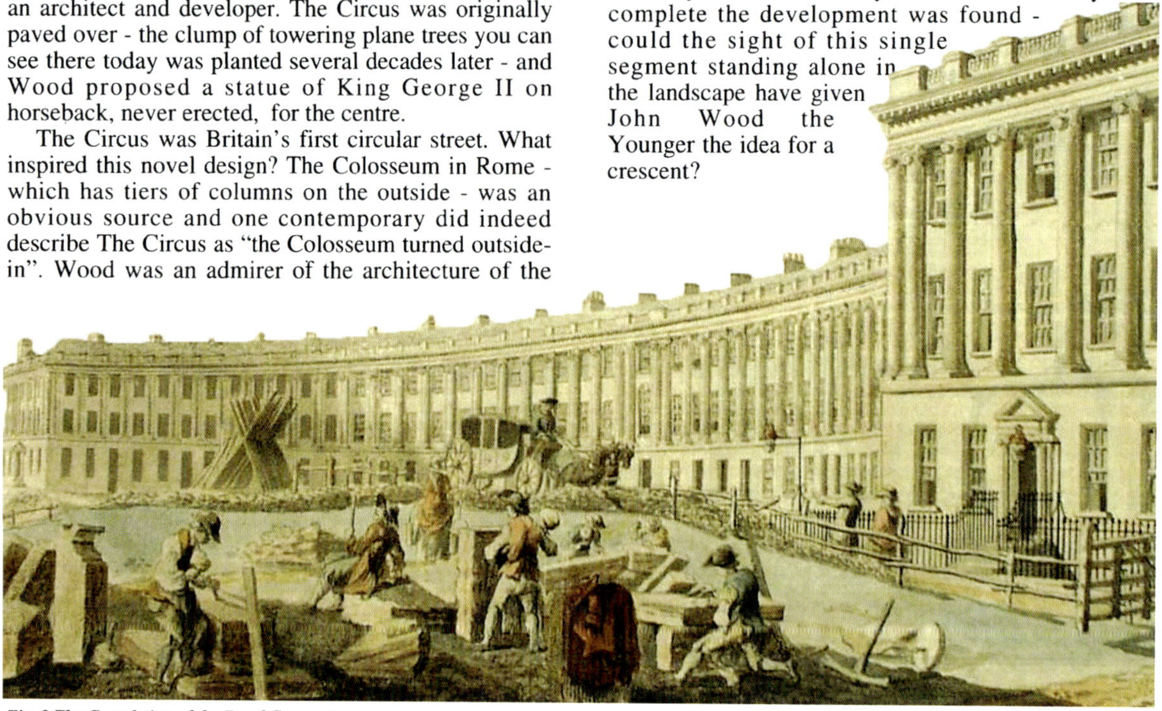

Fig. 3 The Completion of the Royal Crescent
Watercolour by Thomas Malton, 1769

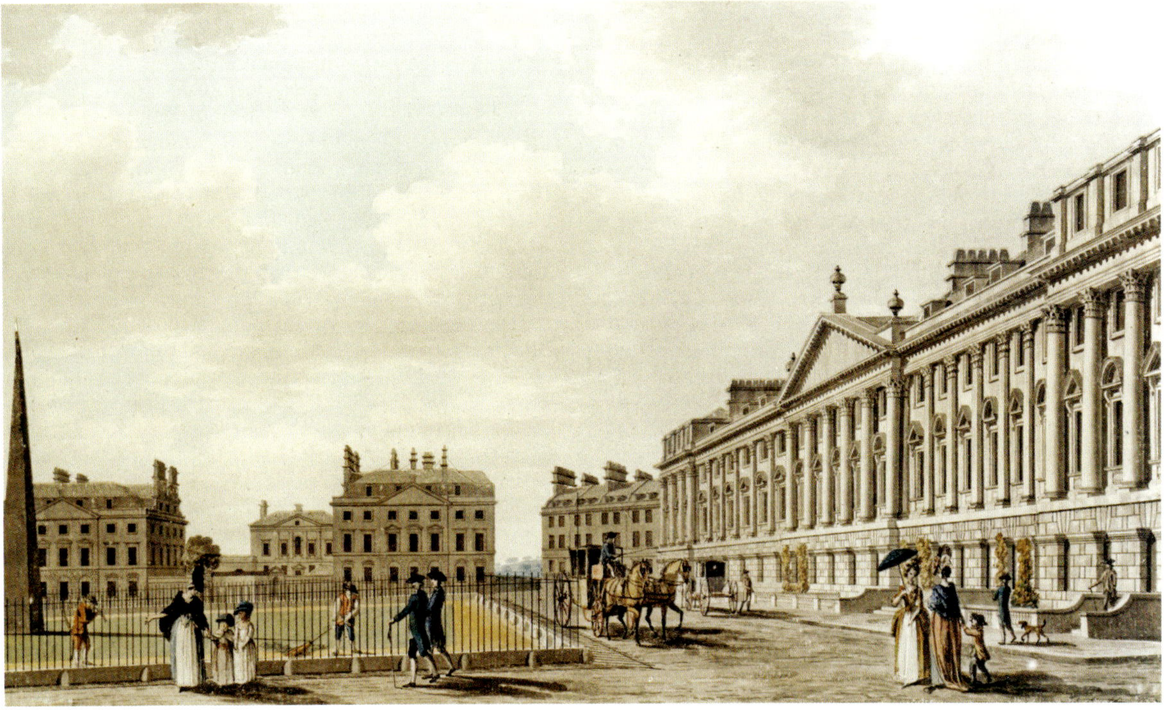

Fig.1 Queen Square
Watercolour by Thomas Malton, 1784. The north side of the square is on the right of the picture.

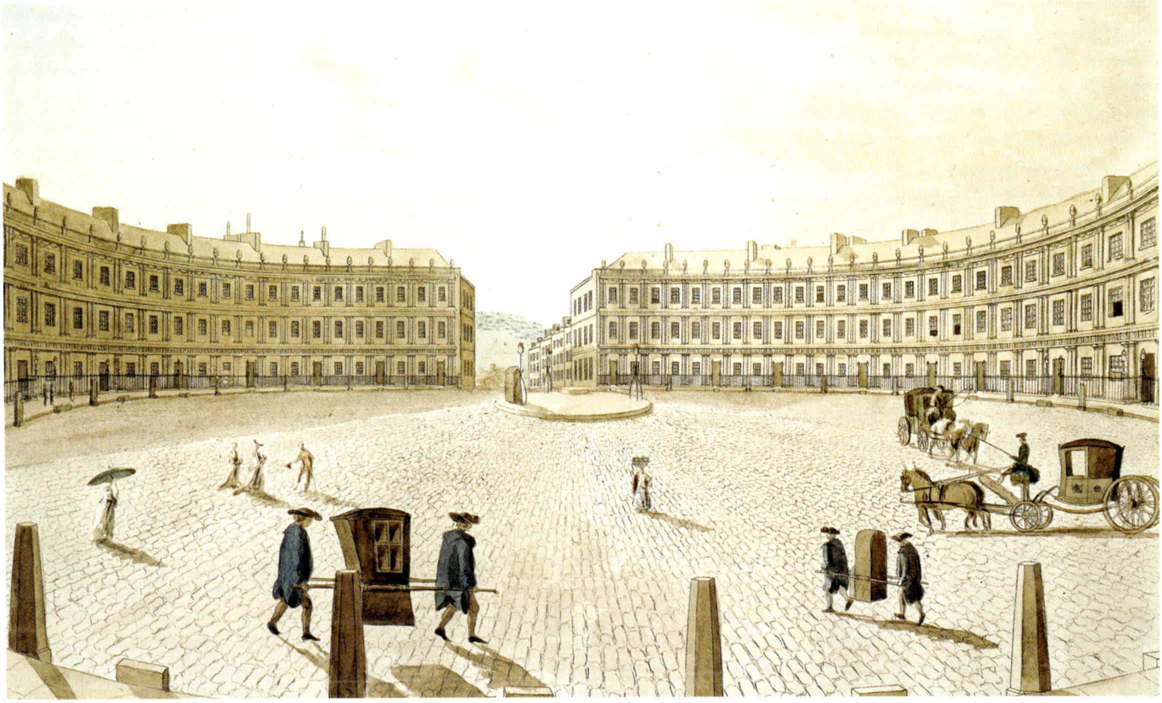

Fig. 2 The Circus
Etching by John Robert Cozens, 1773

The Classical Style

The distinctive style of architecture which John Wood the Elder introduced to Bath had its roots in the classical civilisations of ancient Greece and Rome.

Fig. 1 illustrates a Roman temple "portico", in this case the east front of the Temple of Sulis Minerva at Bath. *Fig. 2* shows the central part of the north side of Wood's Queen Square. Do you see how a Roman portico has been applied to a terrace of houses? Why did architects of John Wood's time follow the architectural style of these vanished civilisations?

Classical architecture, based on principles of symmetry, proportion and the "Five Orders", originated in Ancient Greece and developed throughout the Roman Empire. In Western Europe the style was all but buried during the Dark Ages but it was revived a thousand years later in the Italian Renaissance of the 15th century, the "rebirth" of classical culture. The scholars and architects who examined and measured Roman ruins formed their own theories on the basis of these discoveries and constructed new buildings inspired by these antique exemplars.

Britain shared this reverence for the civilisations of Greece and Rome and the belief that classical architecture was the supreme model. Since Elizabethan times classical ornaments had been applied to buildings as fashionable decorations but in the early 18th century there was a concerted attempt to rediscover the true principles and deeper logic of the style. It was felt that the buildings and written works of the great Venetian architect Andrea Palladio (1509 - 1580) were the most faithful guide to the true spirit of antiquity and his influence on British architects was so immense that the principal style of this period is known as "Palladian".

Buildings designed for Palladio's Italy had to be adapted to the different climate, lifestyle and building methods of Britain, however. In London, the tall, narrow terraced houses which had been typical since the Great Fire of 1666 *(Fig. 3a)* continued to be built but classical proportions and "Orders" were applied to them *(Fig. 3b)*. John Wood was fortunate to work alongside the leading Palladian architects of the day in London and Yorkshire and imported their architectural style to Bath. It continued as the city's accepted style throughout the century *(Fig. 3c)*.

The two most important principles of the style are illustrated by the facade of No. 33 Northampton Street, *(Fig. 3c)*. The first principle was proportion. Do you see how, for example, the area of the facade between the cornice and the cill-course forms a perfect square? There was an almost mystical belief that certain visual proportions - squares, principally - were the key to architectural beauty and harmony; there were "perfect chords" in music and "perfect proportions" in architecture.

The second ruling principle was the use of the Five Orders. These are the five types of column and the superstructures they support, the Tuscan, Doric, Ionic, Corinthian and Composite *(Fig. 4)* and they can be told apart by their differently carved capitals and their individual proportions. The Orders were applied to a building for decorative purposes - as at The Circus - and also to "order" the design of the facade. At Queen Square *(Fig. 2)* the Corinthian Order was *applied* to the facade; at 33 Northampton Street it was *implied*: the facade has been divided in height according to the divisions of an individual column.

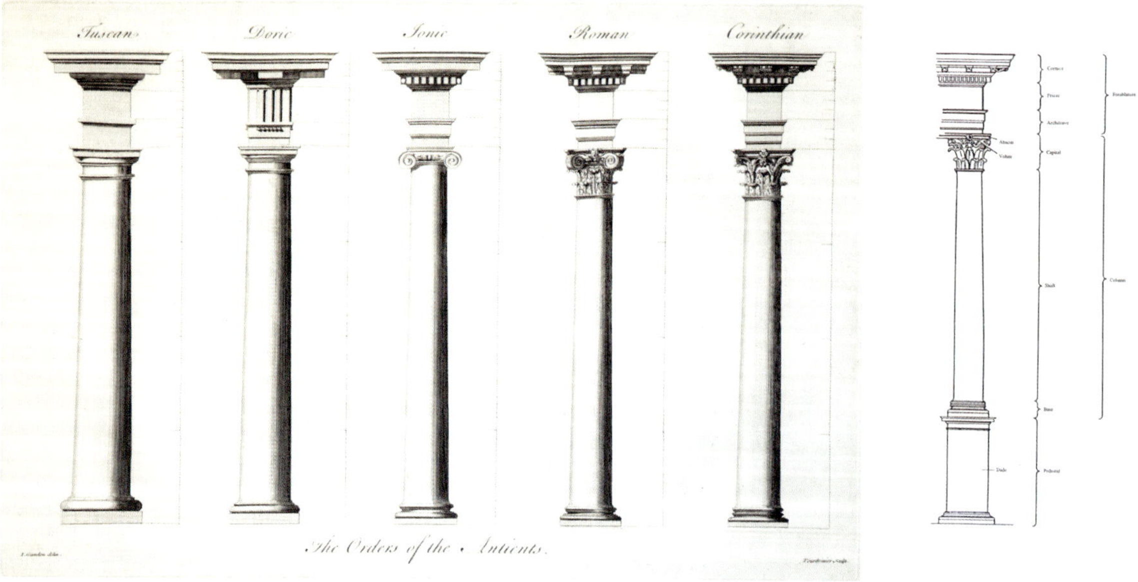

Fig. 4 The Five Orders of Classical Architecture *from William Chambers' Treatise on Civil Architecture, 2nd Ed. 1768*

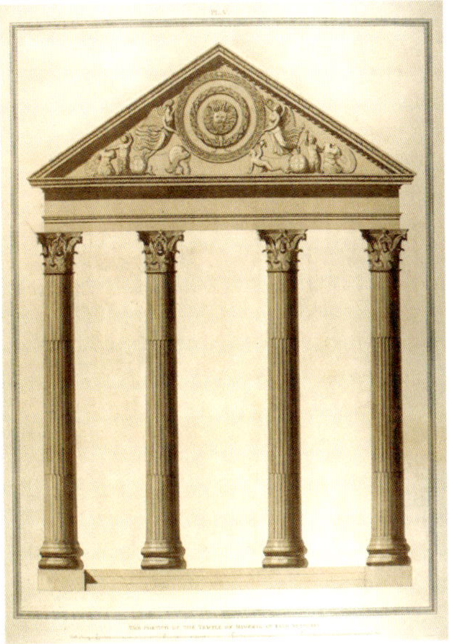

Fig.1 Reconstruction of the east front of the temple of Sulis Minerva in Roman Bath, 1st century AD

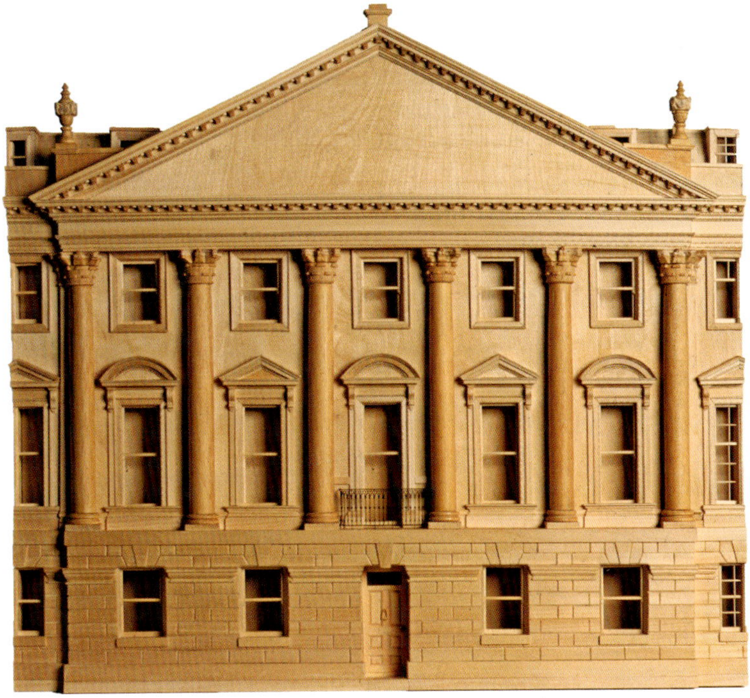

Fig.2 1:25 scale model of 24 Queen Square, c1734

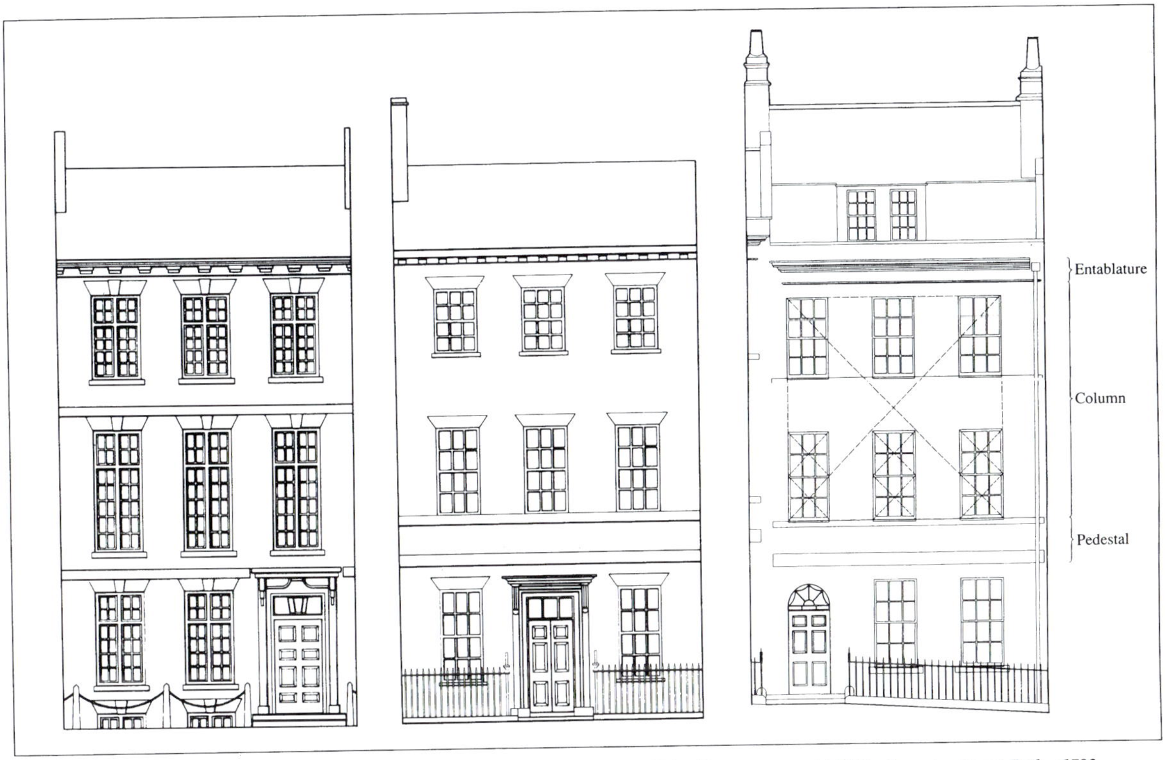

Fig. 3(a) Typical London house 1670 - 1700 (b) Model London house 1750 - 65 (c) 33 Northampton Street, Bath, c1793

Speculative Building

The 18th century was gripped by a passion for gambling and speculative building development offered good odds on making money. This quest for a quick profit had many disadvantages, however, as Matthew Bramble, a disgruntled visitor to Bath in Tobias Smollett's novel *The Expedition of Humphrey Clinker* (1771) points out:

"*...the rage of building has laid hold on such a number of adventurers that one sees new houses starting up... in every corner of Bath; contriv'd without judgement, executed without solidity* [and] *built so slight... that I should never sleep quietly in one of them*".

The vast majority of the new houses built at Bath in the Georgian period were "speculative developments", undertaken in response to the demand for accommodation from the seasonal floods of visitors and the swelling permanent population. The developers and builders were "speculators" because they gambled on finding purchasers for the houses they undertook to construct, and on selling them at a profit.

Whilst in London, John Wood had speculated in building in the booming West End and he was soon looking for a landowner at Bath interested in his schemes. He found one in Robert Gay *(Fig. 1)*, a London surgeon who in 1699 had inherited the Manor of Walcot, an extensive patchwork of small fields to the west and north of the city walls. These were leased to small farmers at trivial rents and, like other landowners, Gay saw building development as a way of reaping a higher yearly yield from his land. He agreed to lease a large plot to John Wood for the latter to build Queen Square upon in return for paying a fixed annual rent of £137 a year, a responsibility passed on to his heirs. The lease lasted for 99 years - the most common length of time - and when it expired all the houses on the site were to become the freehold property of Gay's descendants. Furthermore, once The Square was built more of the family's land lay ripe for development *(Fig. 2)*.

John Wood, being both an architect and developer, designed The Square himself but other developers came from all walks of life - they were physicians, lawyers, businessmen and in some cases landowners developing their own property. They would have to hire an architect to draw up plans and to divide the site up into individual house plots.

The next stage was for the developer to "sub-lease" *(Fig. 3)* these plots to less wealthy speculators, most of whom were building tradesmen. These signed an agreement to construct a house on the plot within a given period - normally two years - during which time they only paid a token "peppercorn rent". Few of these small speculators had enough capital to pay for the construction so they borrowed the money from a wealthy private individual or a bank. When the shell of the house was complete the speculator looked for a buyer, often by advertising in the newspapers *(Fig. 4)* If he failed to find one he faced bankruptcy, but in most years of the 18th century the Bath housing market was buoyant enough for him to sell at a price that repaid the loan and rewarded him with a tidy profit.

The buyer paid a lump sum which was for the shell of the house and for the lease on the plot. He also took on the responsibility of paying the developer the fixed annual rent and if he sold the property on to a new occupier the latter continued to pay it. This is how the developer gained his reward. The rents from the 75 houses in and around Queen Square added up to £305 each year giving Wood, once he had subtracted the £137 rent he owed Gay, a handsome annual profit of £168.

The two Woods left Bath a legacy of over two hundred fine buildings but John Wood the Younger died overburdened by the debts he and his father had accumulated, and his widow ended her life in poverty.

a fire in the room, where perſons are electrified medically.

TO be SOLD by PRIVATE CONTRACT,
By Mr. PLURA,
An elegant ſubſtantial-built HOUSE, ſituated in an open airy part of Bath. The premiſes contain five papered garrets, two attick bed-chambers, two withdrawing rooms, a ſpacious dining-parlour 28 feet by 19, with four windows in front, together with a ſtudy, parlour, and two dreſſing-rooms, an airy Portland ſtone ſtair-caſe and hall, with well planned lower offices, and roomy dry cellars. The whole has lately been fitted up, poſſeſſes every requiſite fixture, and may be taken into poſſeſſion at Lady-Day next.

Full particulars may be known by applying to Mr. Plura.

N. B. To be Lett on Leaſe, *Ready Furniſhed*, in April next, a very convenient HOUSE in AXFORD's-BUILDINGS, commanding an open view of the country. [3398

Fig. 4 Advertisement from "Bath Chronicle", 1790

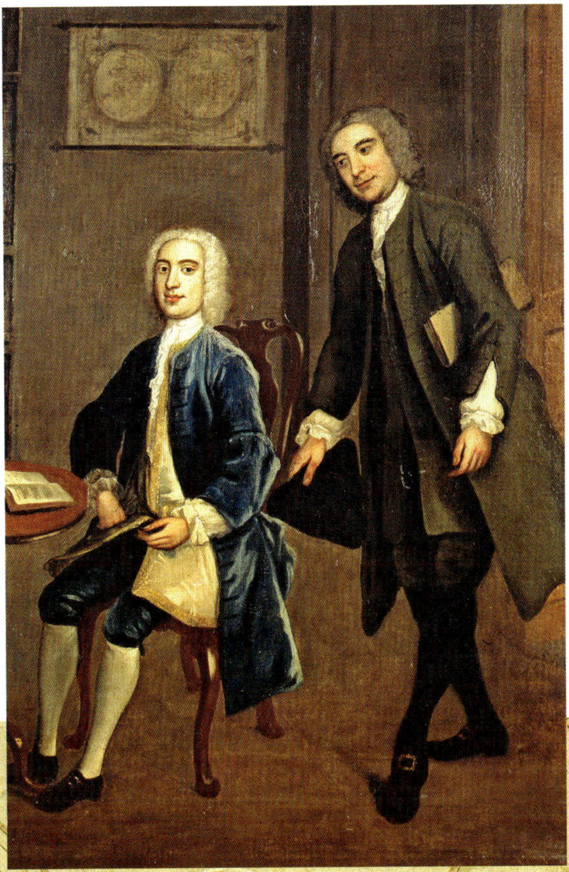

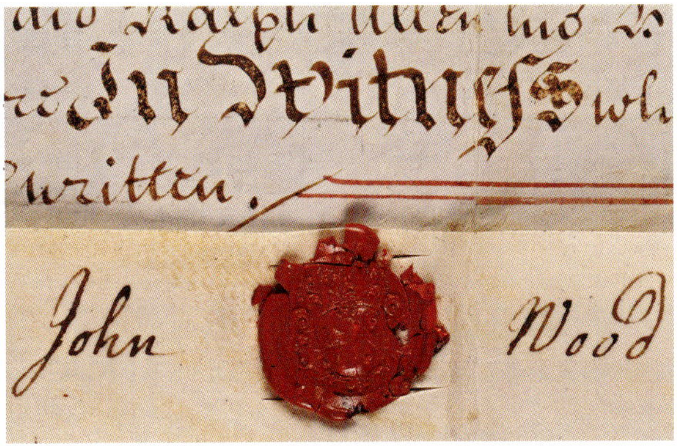

Fig. 3 John Wood's signature and seal on a building agreement

Fig. 1 Robert Gay, Lord of the Manor of Walcot (left) and John Wood (right)
Detail from an anonymous painting

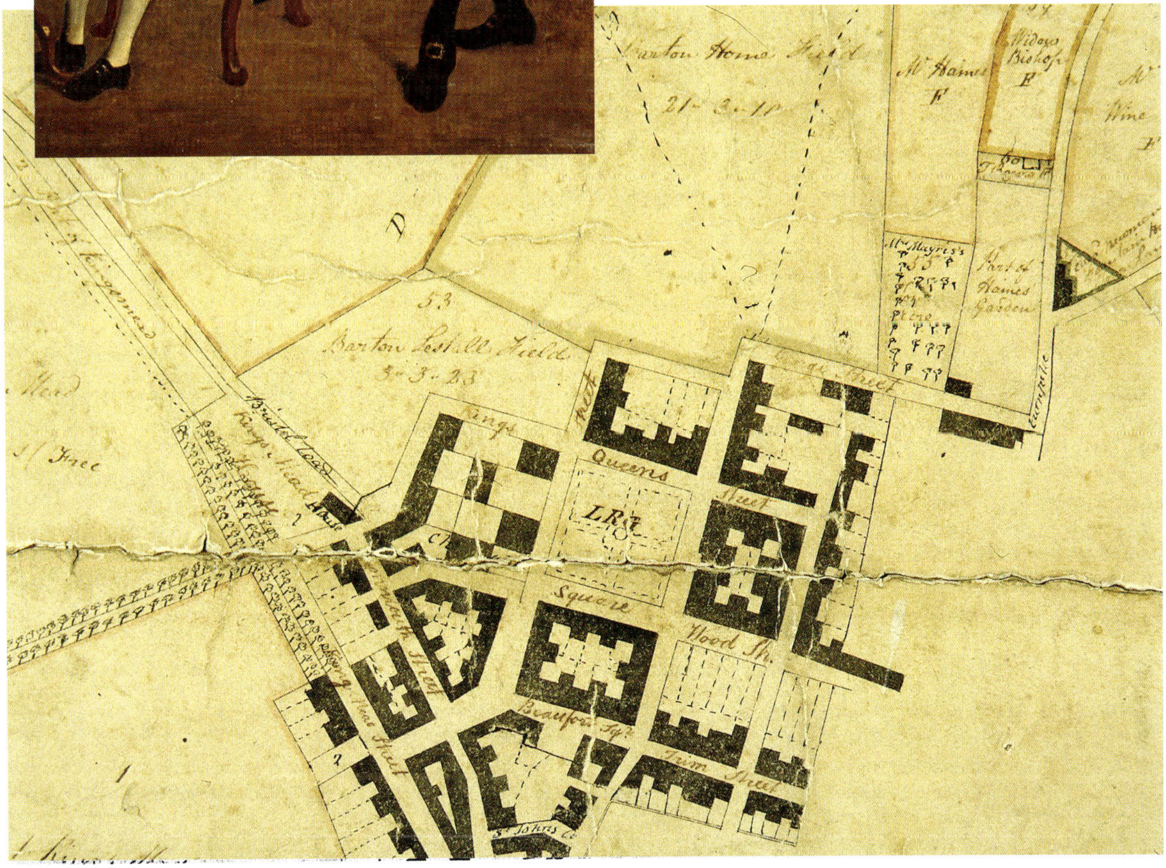

Fig. 2 A Plan of the Parish of Walcot in 1740
Detail showing Queen Square and the farmland belonging to the Manor of Walcot

The Architect and the Design

Architecture was regarded as a science, building as a trade. "Architect" was a prestigious title and the mark of a gentleman. There was no professional qualification but anyone who claimed to be an architect had to show that he understood the principles of the classical style and display his knowledge of geometry, mathematics, sound construction and the latest fashions. It was important that he could furnish the developer with accurate drawings, and drawing instruments were the symbol of the profession *(Fig. 1)*.

John Wood was Bath's first true architect. His rivals in early Georgian Bath had, like him, begun as building tradesmen but they lacked his understanding of the science of architecture. Later generations of architects started out as assistants to older practitioners

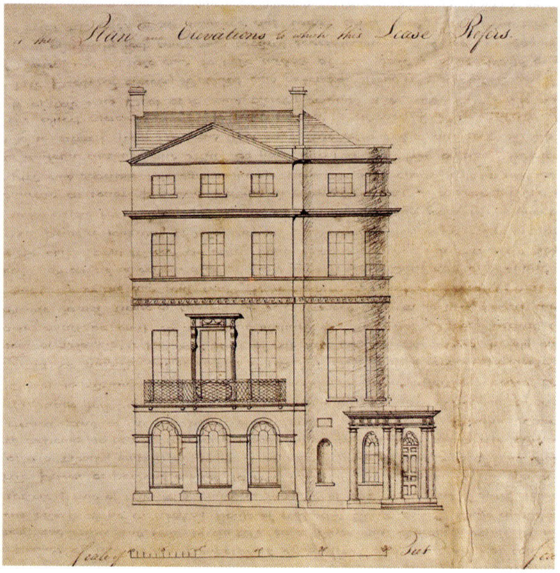

Fig. 4 Building lease for the first house in New Sydney Place, 1808
Detail showing front elevation

but their careers were still founded in the rough and tumble of the building trades. Family connections, political influence and a good grasp of business affairs were also essential to their success. It is unlikely that we would ever have heard of John Wood if he had not been a successful developer as well as a skilled architect.

However, many fine Georgian buildings were designed by "master builders" who did not call themselves architects. These were prosperous, practical men who relied on their long experience and the many "pattern books" published in the 18th century. These books were written specifically for builders and their workmen and displayed page after page of alternative designs for the different elements of the house *(Fig. 2)*. For example, the windows at No. 19 The Vineyards *(Fig. 3)*, near this Museum, seem to have been copied from the book illustrated in *Fig. 2*. Master builders were also able to look at buildings in Bath recently erected by respected architects. They and their workmen had a businesslike approach to building and selling houses and would follow whichever style was in fashion. This helps to explain why the buildings of Georgian Bath are so uniform in appearance.

Developers were equally businesslike. Their most important consideration was that the houses should sell for good prices to prestigious clients. They expected their architects to design houses that were distinguished and modern in appearance and which

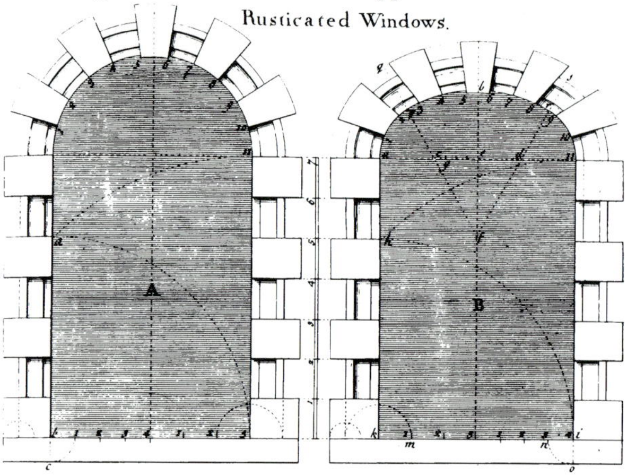

Fig. 2 Design for windows in Batty Langley's The Treasury of Designs, 1756

satisfied the Palladian taste for order and uniformity. However, the more ambitious developments needed to stand out, and here the architect was given the chance to display his originality and flair.

As order and uniformity were such important considerations, each individual builder agreed to construct the front elevation of his house to the architect's design. It became customary for this design to be drawn on the back of the lease *(Fig. 4)*. It was not unknown for builders to bluntly ignore their legal commitments, however, and part of an architect's function was to see that his designs were followed in practice. The building leases' control over design did not normally extend beyond the facade. Although the architect would sometimes be paid a small extra sum to draw up a room plan or particular ornamental details, the interior and rear elevation were generally the work of the builder, his workmen and whoever purchased the house.

This practice ensured that no two interiors in Georgian Bath were ever exactly the same, however similar their facades might be. Another variation you might notice is in the design of the doorcases. The builder or his client were often permitted to replace a plain doorcase with a more elaborate or prestigious design of their own choice. Gay Street has a delightful variety of such ostentatious "home improvements" *(Fig. 5)*.

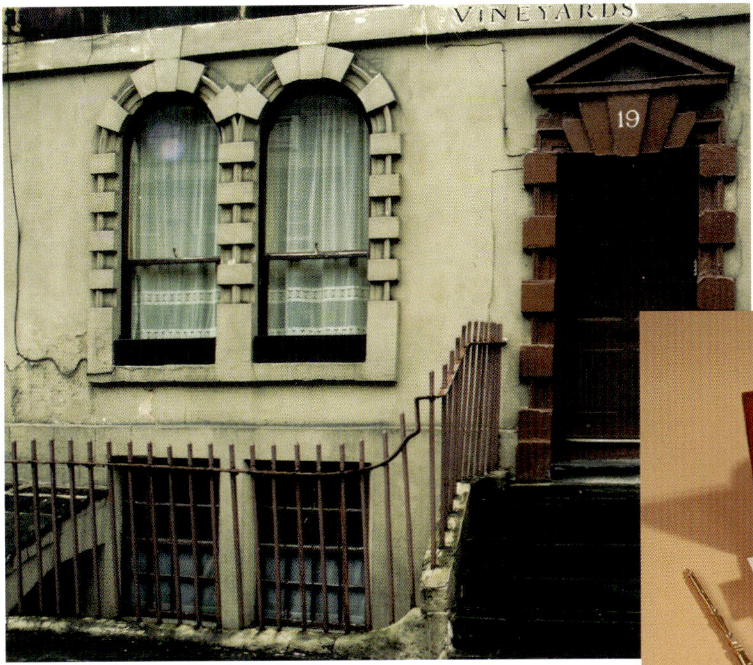

Fig. 3 Windows at No.19 The Vineyards

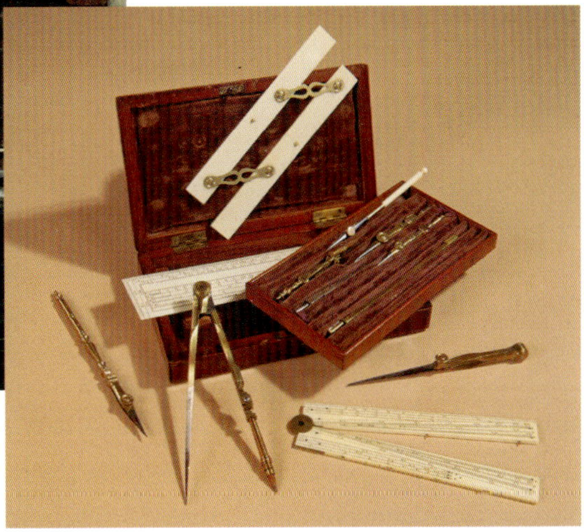

Fig 1. Architect's Drawing Instruments
Brass and ivory in mahogany case, c1830

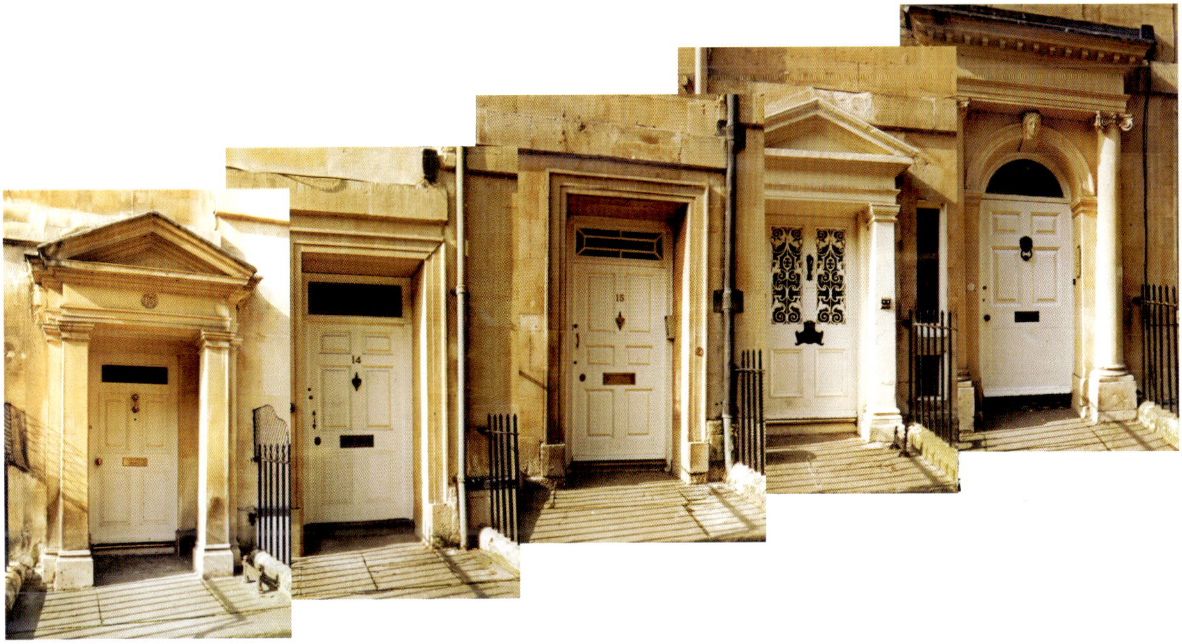

Fig. 5 Doorcases of 13 - 17 Gay Street, Bath

Surveying and Levelling the Land

The developer was responsible for surveying the land, setting out the plots and preparing the site for building. The first step was for hired labourers to lay the "Grand Common Sewer" down the middle of the proposed street. This arched stone channel, normally about five feet high, carried away rainwater, not foul sewage, and initially it also served to drain the site *(Fig. 1)*.

The developer's architect would often act as his surveyor also and would no doubt have learned the necessary skills of measurement and assessment in the same way as he acquired his architectural knowledge - from practical experience and instructional manuals.

The surveyor had to master a number of instruments ranging from simple measuring rules to the theodolite *(Fig. 2)*, an adjustable brass telescope used to set out the angles of the ground plan. When John Wood the Younger set out the building line of Royal Crescent, for example, a theodolite was mounted on a stone pillar erected in the fields below.

John Wood originally hoped to build on the low level plain between the Abbey area and the River Avon, and if his proposals had been accepted Bath might have expanded in that direction. Instead Wood built Queen Square on Robert Gay's estate on the other side of the city, as we have seen, and the success of this scheme encouraged further developments in this northerly direction.

The problem was that the land rose steeply and it was very difficult to create level sites for the houses. *Fig. 3* shows some of the ways in which the builders overcame this problem. The houses stand on man-made platforms which were partly dug out of the hillside and partly raised up on stone vaults. The sudden changes of level and the towering height of the sheer stone walls added to the drama of the architecture and residents of the expanding "Upper Town" enjoyed fresh air and fine "Picturesque" views.

But levelling the site was expensive, troublesome and even dangerous. Camden Crescent *(Fig 4.)*, begun in 1788, was built in a breathtaking position on an eyecatching bluff above the river valley, but the ground proved to be treacherous. As the work neared completion the five houses at the eastern end collapsed and slid down the hill! The crescent was never finished and this explains why the pediment is now not in the centre.

The ancient practice of building houses on stone cellars even on flat, firm sites continued in Georgian Bath. Following the London practice the basement was not excavated to any depth but built up above the ground, probably to keep the kitchens and the goods stored there dry *(Fig. 5)*. The pavement had to be raised to the level of the front door by constructing stone vaults; it was called a "terrass", later giving its name to our modern word "terrace". The level of the road was in turn built up by extending these vaults or filling in with earth. You are quite likely to be standing on a man-made platform wherever you are in Georgian Bath; only the back gardens of the houses remain at their natural level.

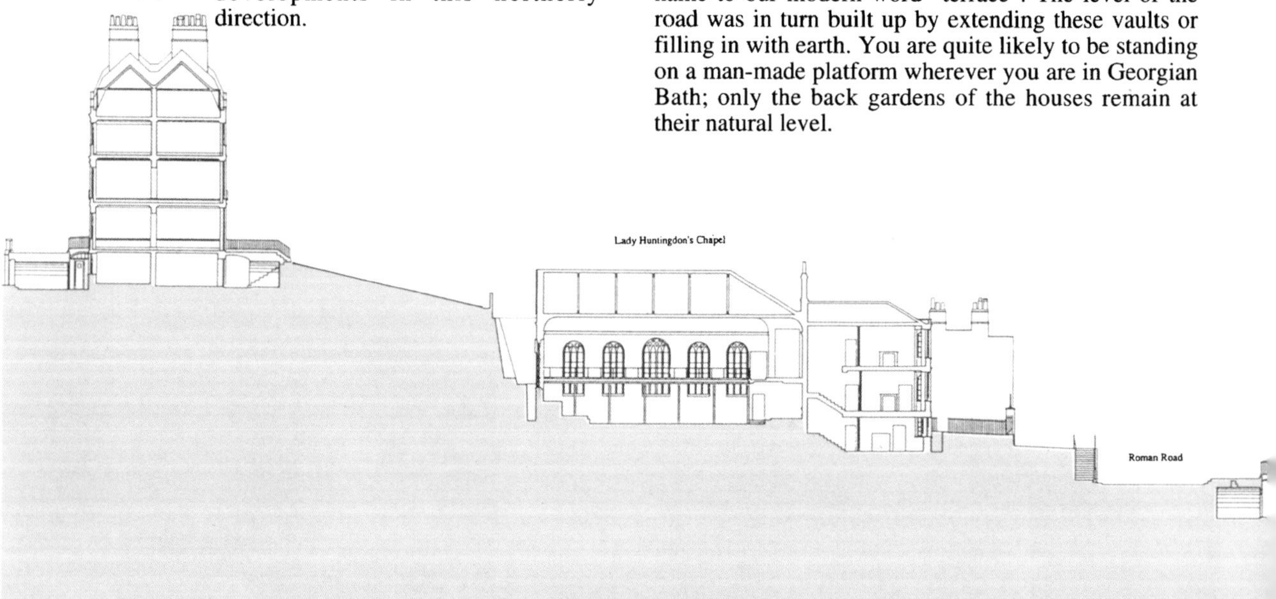

Fig. 3 Cross section from Lansdown Road to the River Avon

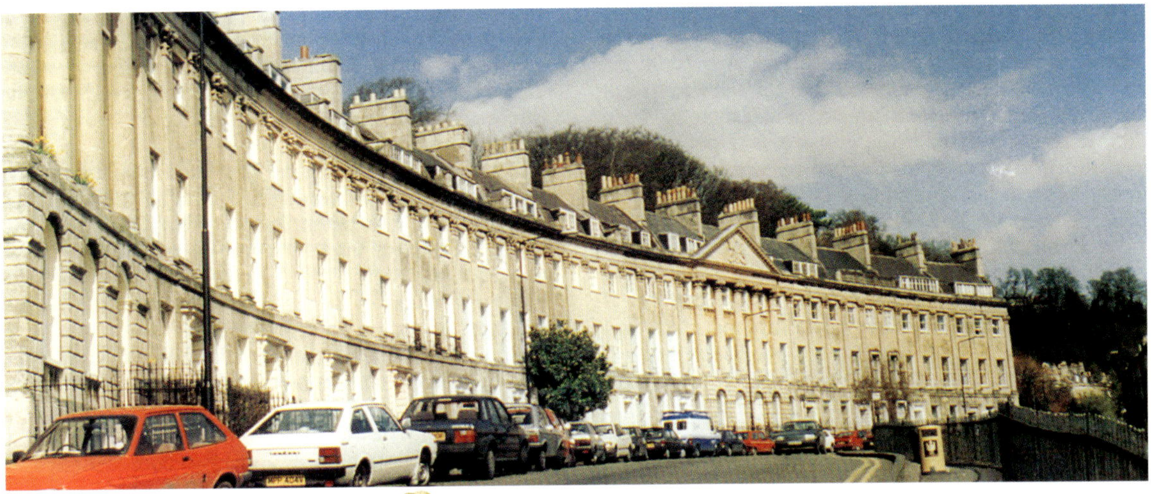

Fig. 4 Camden Crescent

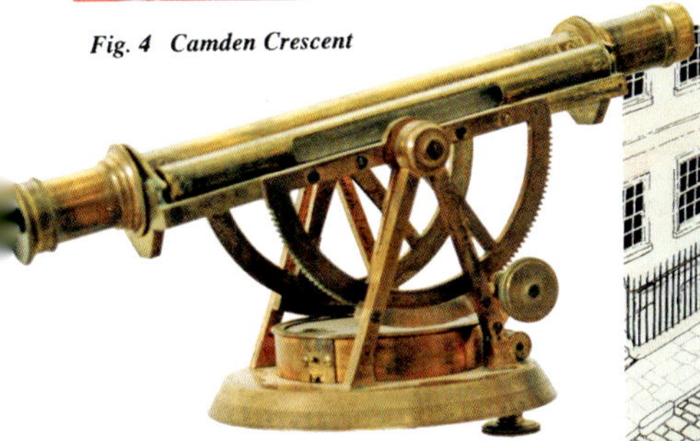

Fig. 2 Brass theodolite
Made by John King of Bristol, late 18th century

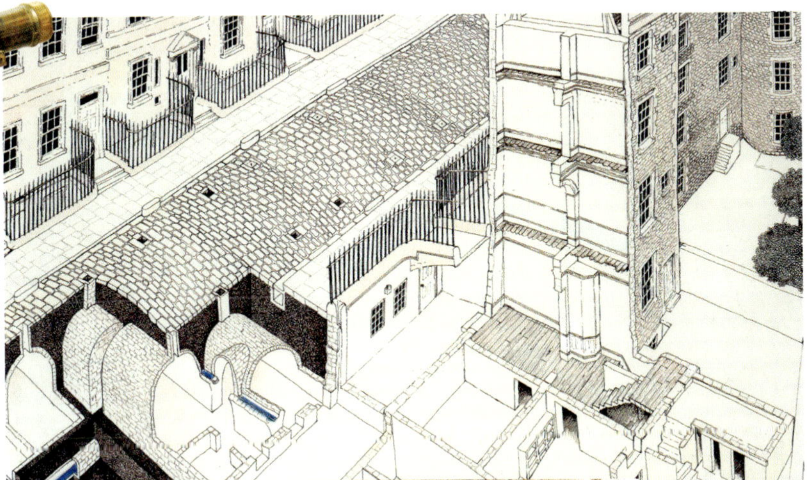

Fig. 5 A view of Gay Street revealing the cellars, vaulting and Grand Common Sewer

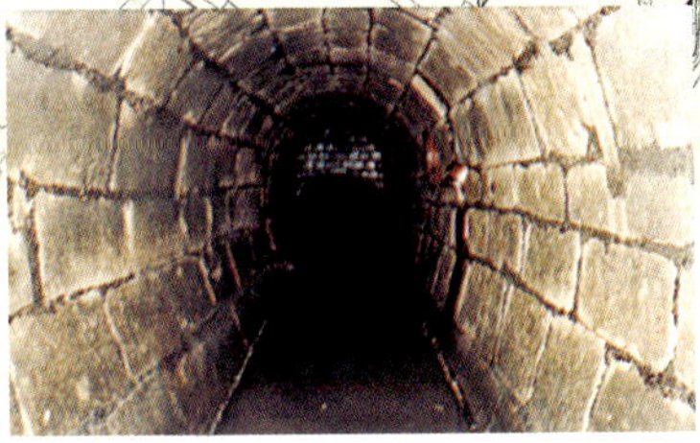

Fig. 1 Grand Common Sewer, Avon Street

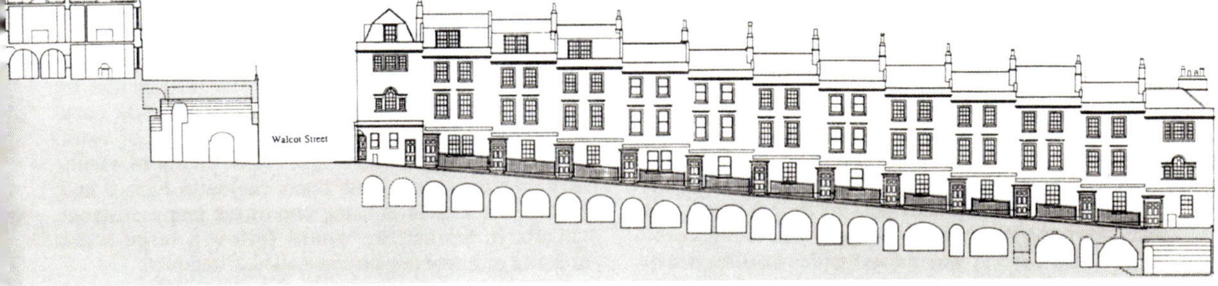

Stone

Building materials were the greatest expense the speculative builders faced, costing far more than the labour, so they tended to use as little as they could get away with. We must remember that they aimed to sell the completed house for a lump sum and then leave, so they were not worried if the property was poorly built and did not survive the length of the lease. The developer and landowner saw the property as a long term investment, however. Their heirs would collect rents for the full length of the lease, 99 years in most cases, and when the lease expired the houses would fall into the hands of the landowner's descendants - if they were still standing! They made sure that the leases the builders signed laid down certain standards of construction. The developer's surveyor would inspect the house to check that the builders were obeying them.

At the beginning of our period building materials had to come from sources near to Bath because the route down the River Avon to Bristol and the seaborne trade routes beyond was unnavigable; hauling heavy loads long distances over the poor roads of the time was too expensive. In 1726 - 7 the Avon Navigation Company constructed several locks and cut a short canal, dug under John Wood's supervision. A wider variety of plentiful building materials could now be imported from Bristol and its trading partners further afield.

Soft, mellow limestone has been quarried in the Bath area since Roman times but the industry was small until 1726 when Ralph Allen (1693 - 1764) began to buy up land for quarries on Combe Down, overlooking Bath to the south. Allen had already made a fortune by reorganising the country's postal services; he was a remarkable businessman who was also a great patron of John Wood, Alexander Pope and numerous charitable works in the city.

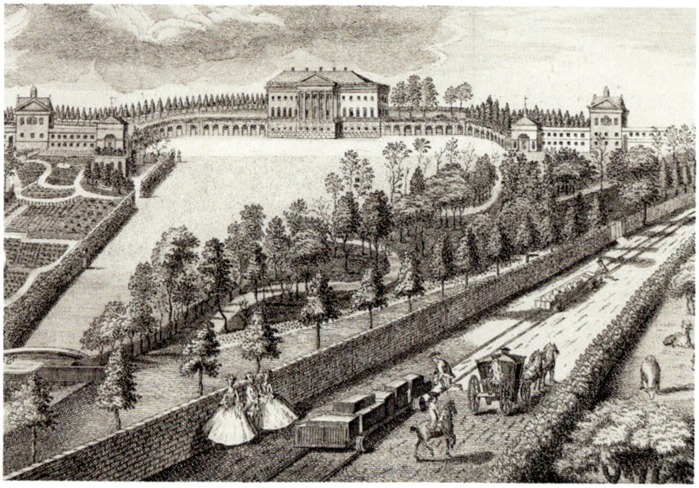

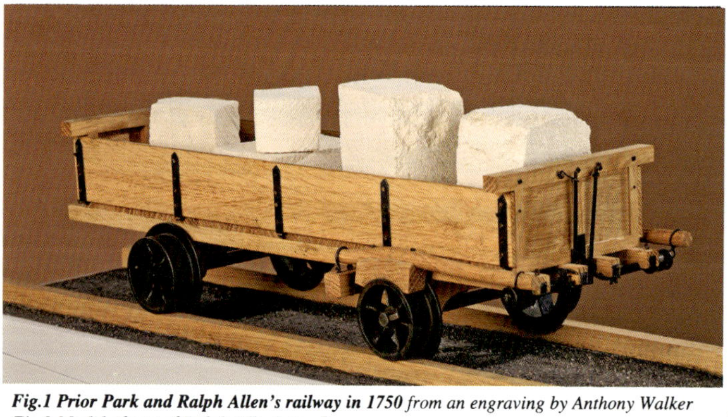

Fig.1 Prior Park and Ralph Allen's railway in 1750 *from an engraving by Anthony Walker*
Fig.2 Model of one of Ralph Allen's trucks

Allen's next step was to employ the Bristol engineer John Padmore to invent an ingenious railway for him *(Fig. 1)*. The stone from the earlier quarries on the hills had trundled down the steep slope to the river in slow and clumsy horse-drawn carts but now trucks carrying three or four tons at a time rolled down on wooden rails *(Fig. 2)*. The trucks had flanged iron wheels to keep them on the rails, the first known use of this type of wheel. One man operated the mechanical brake and the empty trucks were hauled back up by horses. The railway cut prices for building stone and was such a remarkable innovation for its time that it became a popular attraction for tourists who would also view Allen's mansion of Prior Park, begun to John Wood's designs in 1735 and intended to be an advertisement for the quality of Bath stone. At Allen's riverside stoneyard and wharf *(Fig. 3)* a crane, also cleverly designed by Padmore, loaded the blocks of stone on to barges bound for Bath, or for Bristol - and then from Bristol to London and other markets.

The blocks of stone for buildings in Bath would be cut and "dressed" into shape by masons working at low benches called "bankers" in open shelters called "lodges". The builder contracting for a house would order his stone from these yards, of which Allen's was the largest and best known.

A principal task of the stonemasonry yard was the production of "ashlar", rectangular blocks of stone that were roughly dressed with an axe at the back and sawn smooth at the front. Another type of work was the carving of more decorative pieces of stone, such as the window jamb being carved in *Figs. 4* and 5. Here the mason is using one of the many different chisels in his kit; he would follow a large scale drawing or a wooden outline called a "template".

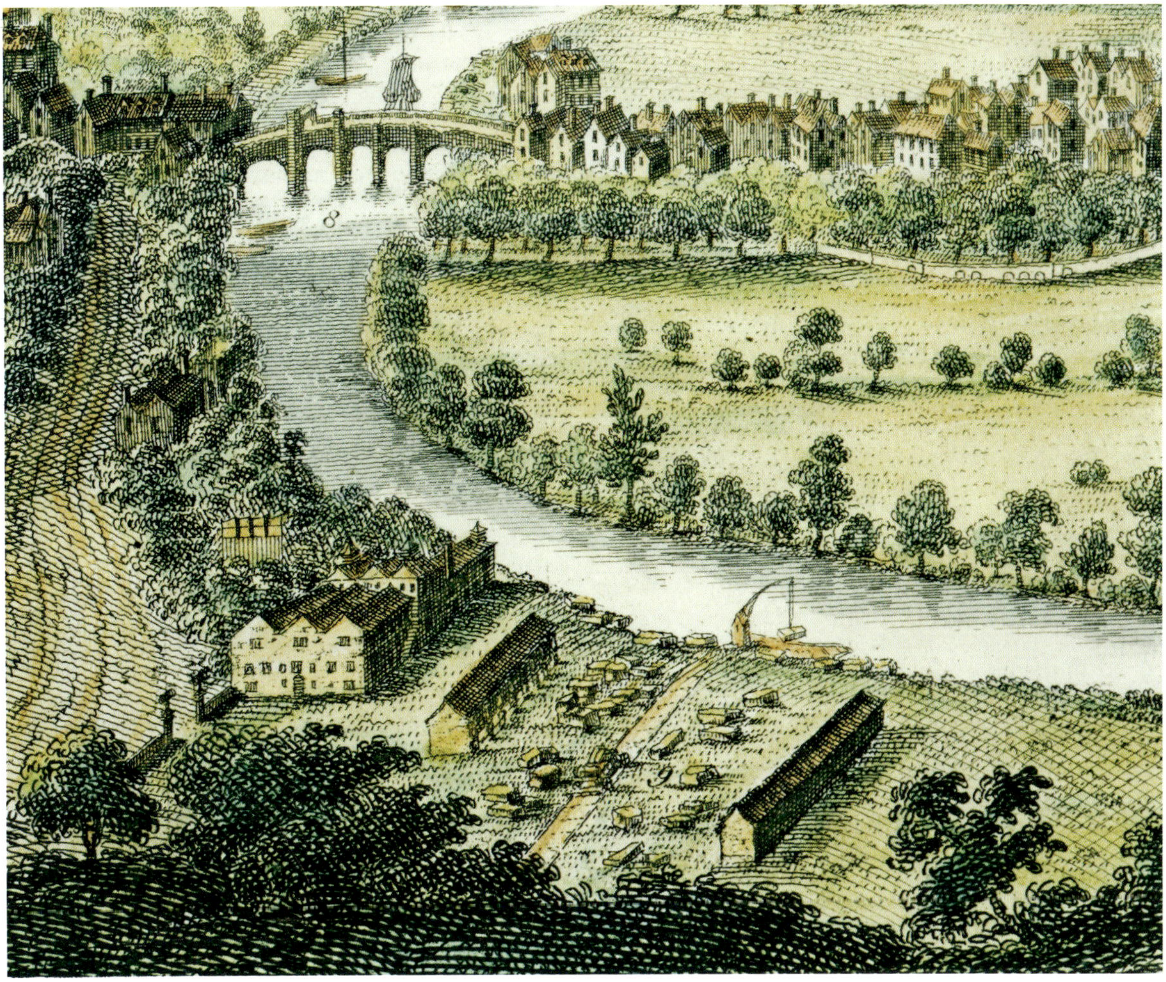

Fig.3 Ralph Allen's stoneyard and wharf at Widcombe
Detail from the Bucks' "South East Prospect of Bath", 1734

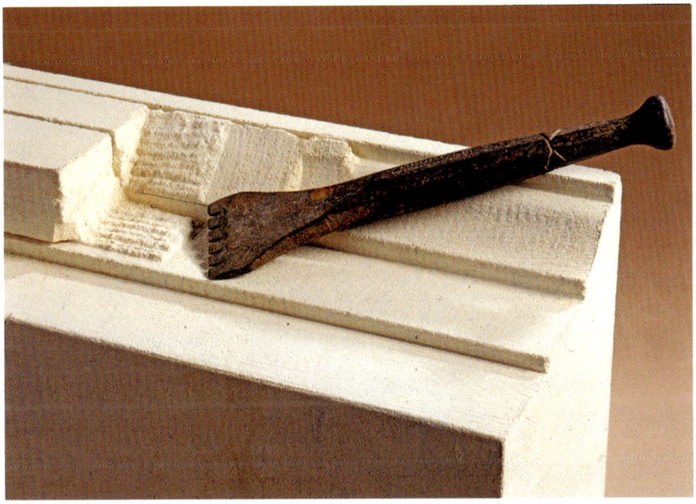

Fig.4 Window jamb in the process of being carved

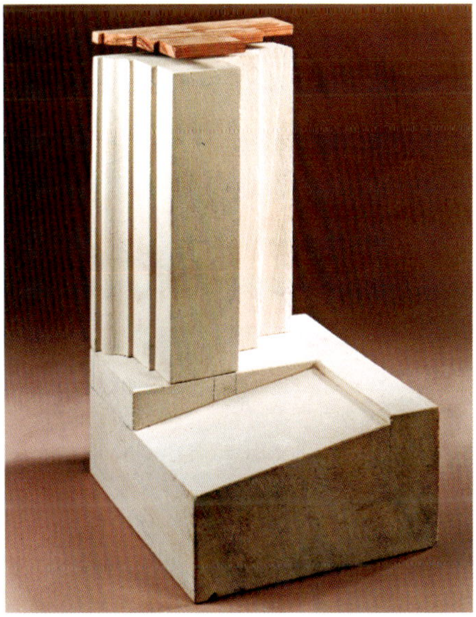

Fig.5 Carved window jamb and cill with wooden template

On site

This fascinating picture *(Fig.1)* was drawn by a touring artist named Samuel Grimm and shows Argyle Street and Laura Place *(Fig.1 insert)* under construction in June 1789.

The masons preparing the stone could work all through the year in their covered lodgings but it was best to stop actual construction work in the winter months because the lime mortar might freeze and crack.

Notice how uneven the progress of the development is. The builders were allowed two years in which to "roof and cover in" - that is, to complete the shell of the house - and each began work when it best suited him. The shell of the house towering over the trees on the right of the picture is complete but the builder next door has not yet started. The latter would pay an agreed proportion of the cost of the shared party wall and the surveyor would settle the disputes that might arise between neighbours over such matters.

A small boat is delivering materials to the wharf beside the old mill; timber is stacked under the trees to the right and stone by the wharf. You can see ladders and wooden scaffolding propped up against an adjacent house. The scaffolding platforms were erected by laying wooden planks over a precarious framework of tall poles lashed together with rope *(Fig.2)*.

Stones were brought up to the platform in a number of ways. Workmen dragged them up the sides of the ladders with rope or carried them on hods and wicker paniers *(Fig. 3)*. Heavier blocks of masonry were lifted up by machines. One that was commonly used is depicted in *Fig 4*. The triangular wooden frame was fixed at an overhanging angle on top of the construction. The two levers turned the wooden barrel, called a "windlass"; as the windlass revolved it wound the rope round over the pulley and this hoisted up the piece of stone on the end. *Fig. 5* shows a more substantial crane which works on the same principle but which would probably only have been used on more impressive buildings.

Building sites were dangerous places. Contemporary newspapers frequently contain accounts of workmen crushed by masonry, buried by earth or fallen from scaffolding or roofs. It seems that few major developments were completed without loss of life.

Building was divided into different trades - masons, carpenters, tilers, glaziers, smiths, plumbers, paviours, joiners, turners, carvers, plasterers and painters. Building tradesmen began their working lives at a young age by choosing a trade and enrolling as an apprentice under an older "Master". After seven years of apprenticeship they were free to leave and look for work and if they were successful might eventually set up as "masters" themselves. Men from all the trades collaborated on each house. Each contracted with the builder for his share and an architect or surveyor might be called in to measure and value the completed work. It was common practice for one tradesman to pay another "in kind" - that is, by carrying out work in return.

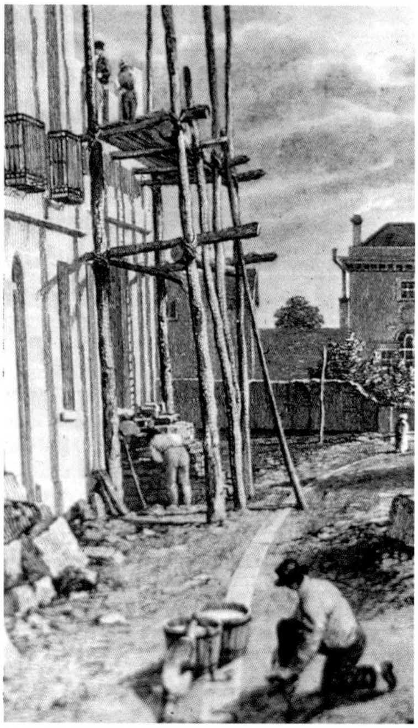

Fig.2 Houses under construction in Beaumont Street, Oxford, 1825 showing typical scaffolding

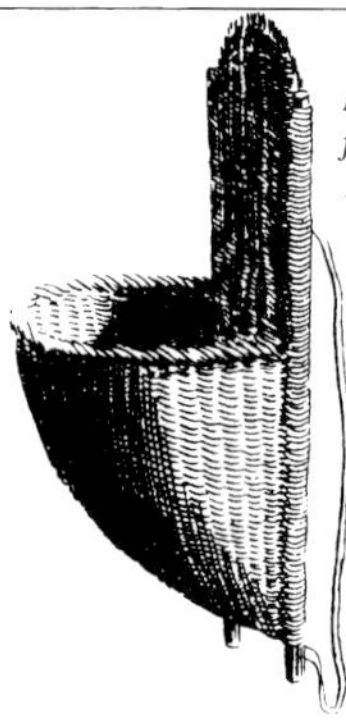

Fig. 3 Mason's wicker panier
from L'Encyclopedie Diderot, Paris 1762 - 77

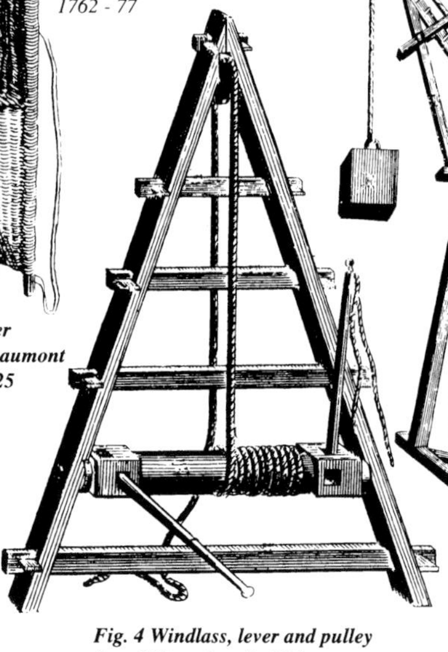

Fig. 4 Windlass, lever and pulley
from L'Encyclopedie Diderot, Paris 1762 - 77

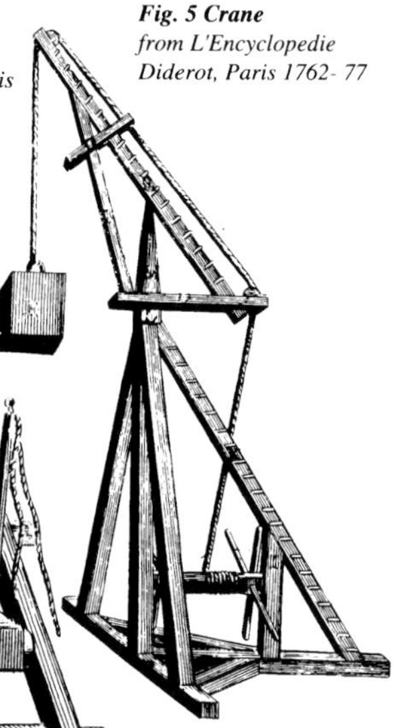

Fig. 5 Crane
from L'Encyclopedie Diderot, Paris 1762- 77

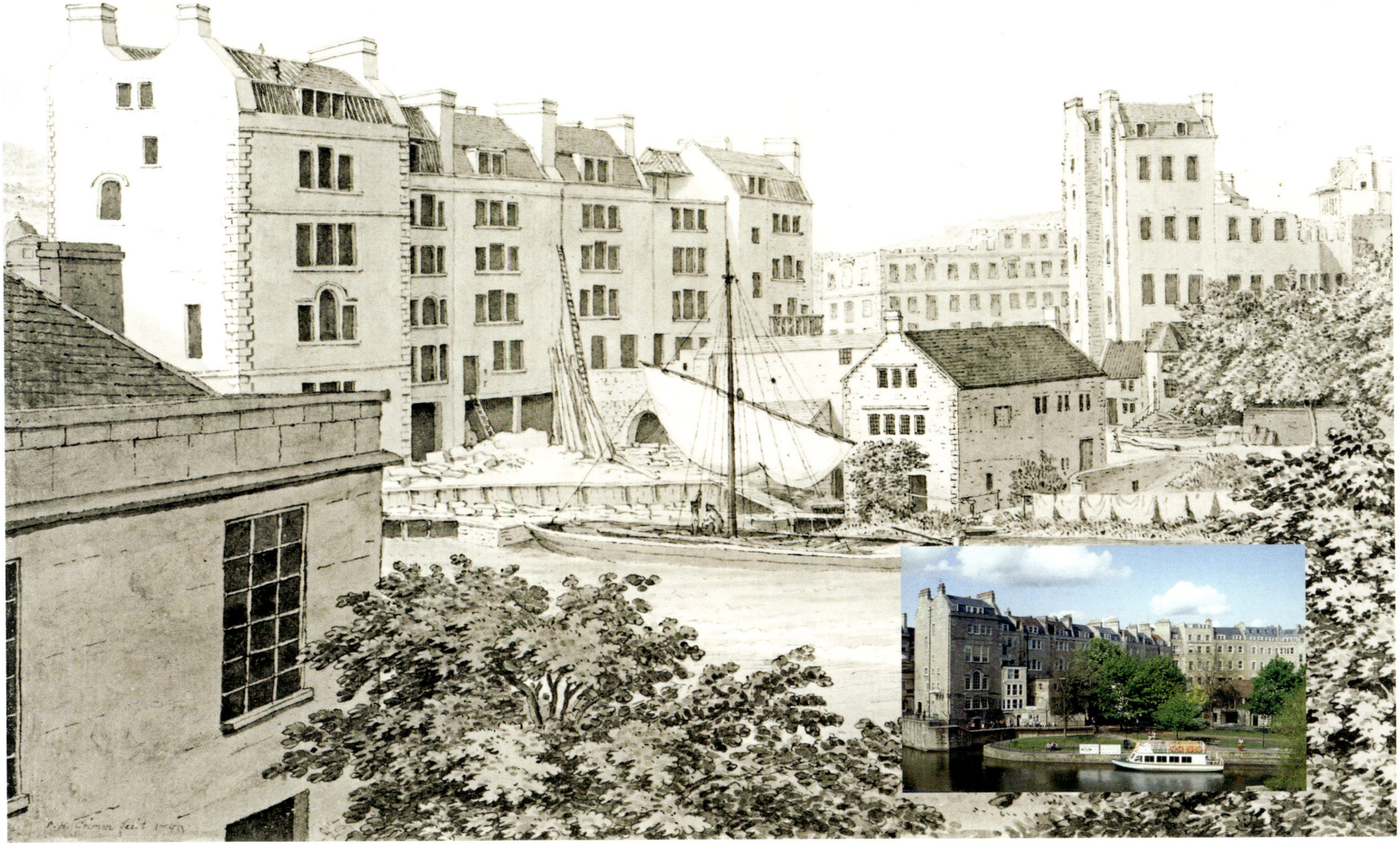

Fig.1 "A View of the New Town in June 1789 taken from a house in Orange Grove" by *Samuel Grimm*
Insert: the same view today

Masonry

The masonry trade in Bath was divided into two branches: the masons who worked the stone into shape in the stoneyards, and those who built the houses with these stones and were known as "rough masons".

The most important wall of the house was the front wall, the "facade", because it faced up to the public *(Fig. 1)*. The ashlar blocks brought from the freemasons' yards were laid in even courses with almost invisible "hairline" mortar joints between them in order to give the wall as even and seamless an appearance as possible *(Fig. 2)*. The entire facade was

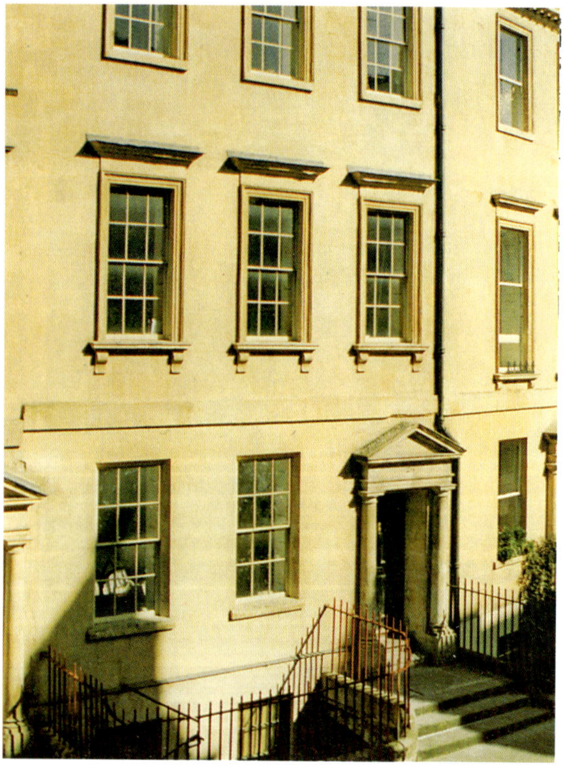

Fig.1 Facade of 26 Rivers Street

combed down with a "mason's drag" to smooth out any blemishes *(Fig. 3)*. The ideal was a facade which almost looked like a single piece of stone. Ashlar was expensive, however, and rubble stone formed most of the wall's thickness *(Fig. 4)*. Rubble was cheaper stone, mostly obtained from certain beds of the quarry or the waste left over when the stone was worked into shape. The rubble and ashlar walls were tied together by the longer "bonding stones" which projected from the ashlar face into the rubble core.

When you remember that most neighbouring houses in a terrace were built by different speculators the smooth transition between their facades seems remarkable. One reason is that the same mason might contract for several neighbouring plots - Samuel Emes, an experienced builder known and trusted by John Wood, contracted for all the rough masonry in Queen Square. Even if this was not the case, it was customary practice to leave alternate courses of ashlar projecting for the masons next door to "tooth in" to. *(Fig. 5)*.

It is common to find cheaper houses in Bath with facades built of nothing more than ashlar blocks, the rubble backing having been omitted in order to cut costs *(Fig. 6)*. The survival of such thin walls is a

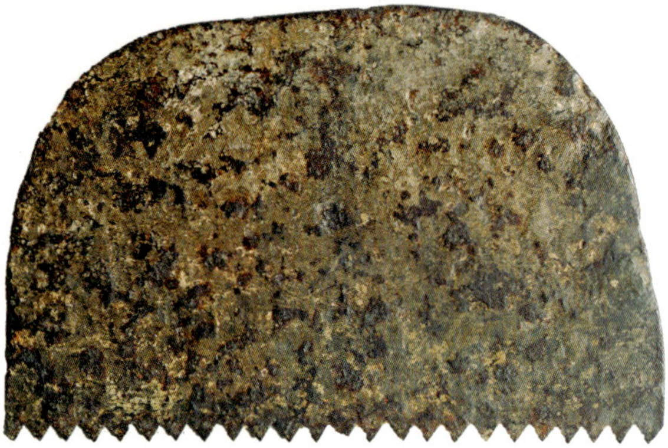

Fig.3 Mason's drag, early 19th century

testament to the masons' skill and their precision in building with ashlar.

Also in *Fig. 6* notice the oyster shell that has been wedged into the mortar joint. Oysters were not a luxury in the 18th century - indeed, they were eaten as snacks almost as packets of crisps are today! - and masons used the shells, or shards of slate, to pack the joint and support the stone until the soft lime mortar had set. Masons used very little mortar - their art lay in building walls that would stand up without its assistance.

It was regarded as good practice to build all the walls of the house at once. The rubble rear walls of Georgian houses in Bath *(Fig. 7)* presented a striking contrast to the smooth and even front elevations. They were only likely to be faced with ashlar if they stood prominently in the view. Otherwise, they were regarded as much less important than the front and only rubble would be used. This was carefully laid in even courses and probably plastered over in order to protect the joints from the weather and give a semblance of uniformity. Bladud's Buildings, a terrace near the Museum, is almost unique in Bath because its rear elevation - a prominent sight from the river valley below - matches its front.

Fig.2 Reconstruction of section of ashlar facade

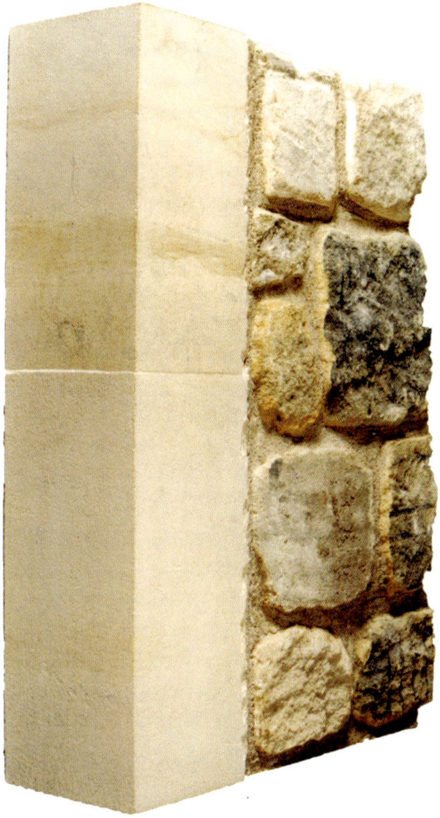

Fig.4 Reconstruction of section through rubble and ashlar wall

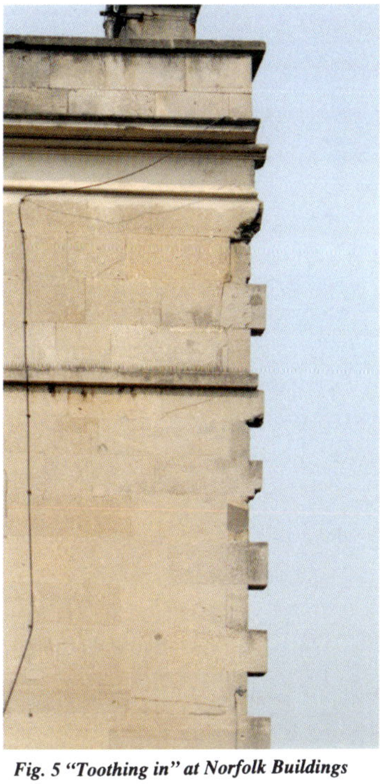

Fig. 5 "Toothing in" at Norfolk Buildings

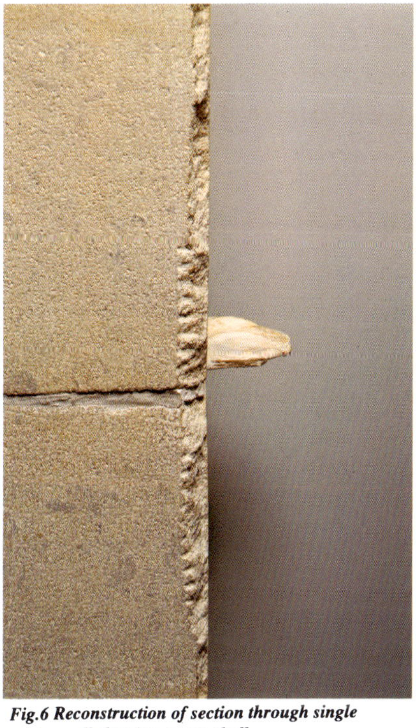

Fig.6 Reconstruction of section through single ashlar wall showing oyster shell

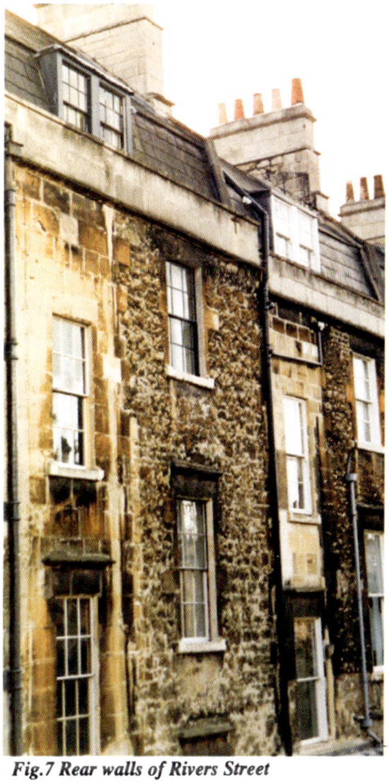

Fig.7 Rear walls of Rivers Street

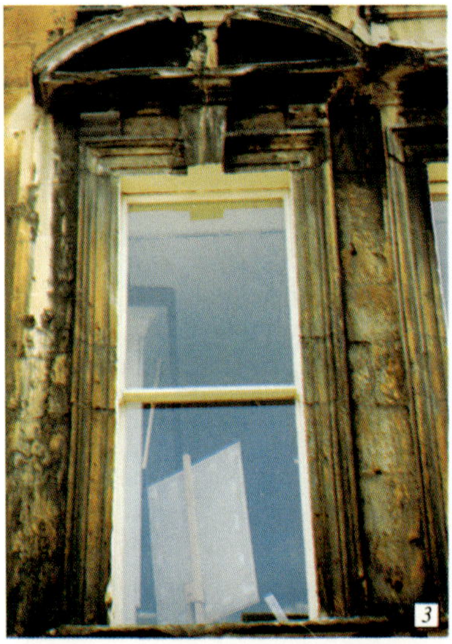
3

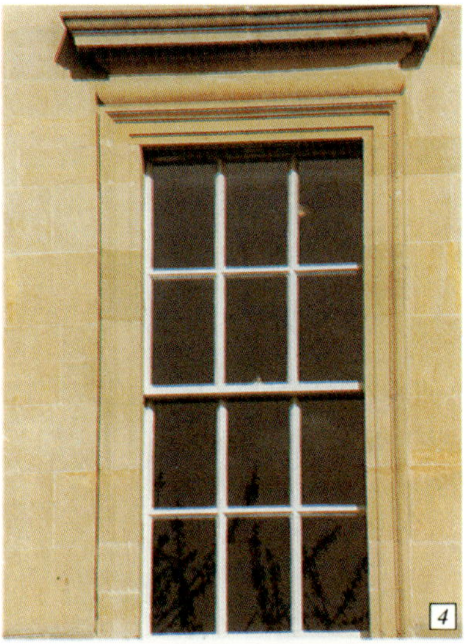
4

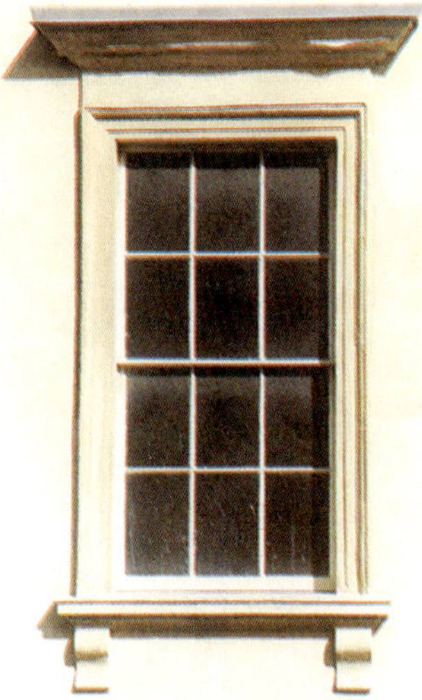
5

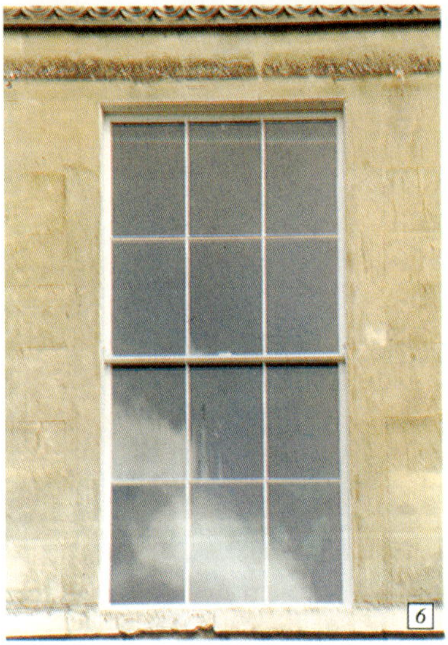
6

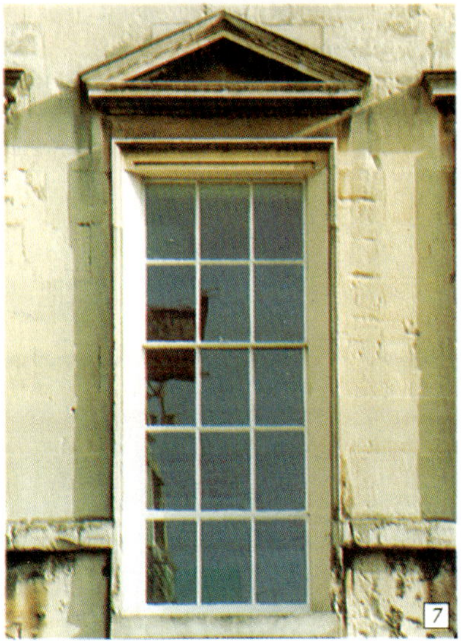
7

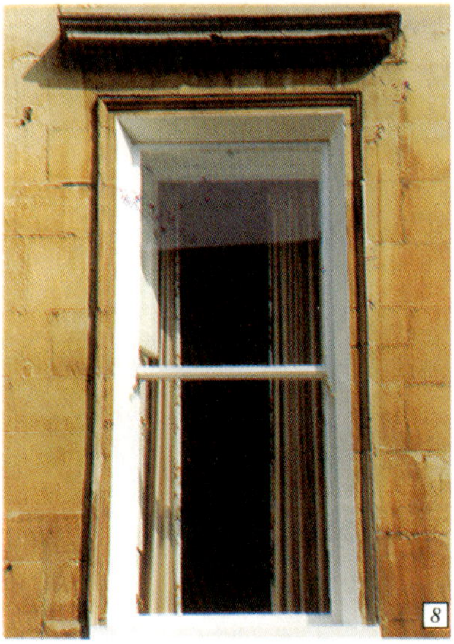
8

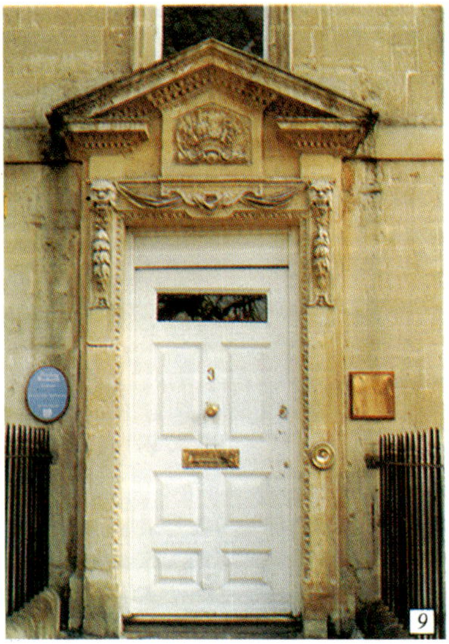
9

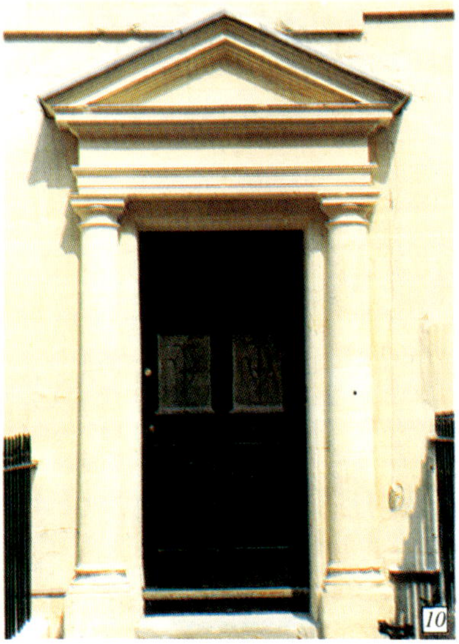
10

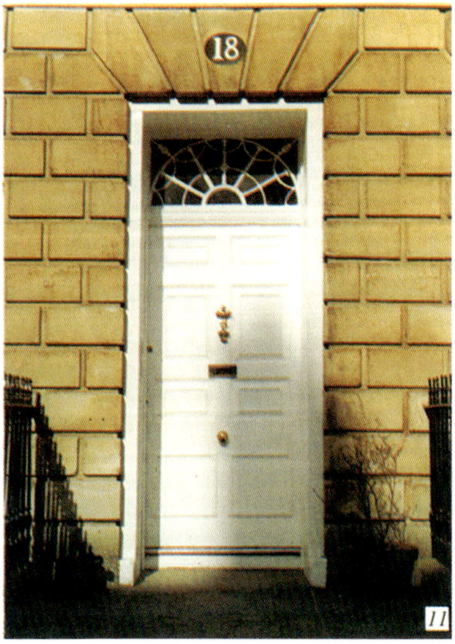

11

Window and Door Surrounds

The stone surrounds to windows and doors are important features of the Georgian facade.

A window surround was formed from a number of blocks of carefully shaped stone which the rough masons set into the wall as it rose *(Fig.1)*. Window openings of average size are spanned by a single block of stone called a "lintel" *(Fig. 1a)*, which supports the wall above, and the uprights of the opening are constructed of "window jambs". The face of a jamb may be enriched with decorations and the back is shaped to accommodate the window. You have seen another jamb being carved in the "Stone" section; *Fig. 2* shows a jamb which has the same carved enrichment as the earlier example and which also bonds into the front wall of the building *(Fig. 1b)*.

The first floor rooms of the Georgian house were the most important and as a result had the most elaborate and prominent window surrounds. The photographs on the facing page have been selected to illustrate the changes in their style during the Georgian period.

At the beginning, stone carvers were at liberty to execute bold, sculptural designs such as the dramatic window at 14 Green Street, c1716 *(Fig. 3)*. *Fig. 4* shows a very different window at 4 Queen Square, c1730. Every crisp detail of this design conformed to the Palladian style and its similarity to the window at 26 Rivers Street *(Fig. 5)*, forty years later in date, illustrates the durability of this influence. These strict standards of taste constrained the carver's style and limited his choice of designs. By the end of the century taste favoured even plainer surrounds, which did not draw attention away from the overall impression of the facade *(Fig. 6)*.

Changes to windows caused by advances in fashion and technology have affected the appearance of Georgian facades more than anything else. Firstly, in the early 19th century there was a fashion for lengthening windows in order to lighten the rooms and open them up to the outside *(Fig. 7)*. An extra row of panes would be added and the window surround extended through the cill-string. The cill-string, the projecting band of stone running beneath the windows, has been left in this instance but was often chiselled off.

Secondly, at some point in the 19th century the edges of the surrounds were tooled - or "chamfered" - off at a 45 degree angle and painted white to allow more light. Thirdly, the window glass itself changed. In the 18th century sheets of glass were limited in size and the window was divided into a number of panes. In the 1830s, however, new technology made large sheets of "cylinder glass" available at affordable prices. The dramatic use of this "improved cylinder sheet glass" at the famous Crystal Palace in 1851 added to its fashionable appeal and it was eventually installed in the front elevation of nearly every house in Bath *(Fig. 8)*.

The window in *Fig. 5* has recently been restored to its original design. The window in *Fig.8* was originally very similar and the difference between the two illustrates the dramatic effect these 19th century alterations had on the appearance of a Georgian facade.

Stone doorcases during the period were designed for architectural effect and personal prestige, not to provide shelter. *Figs. 9, 10* and *11* have been chosen to give you an impression of the changes in their style which, broadly speaking, developed in a similar way to that of windows in the city. The first is a flamboyant display of a stone carver's unfettered skill; the second, executed to a standard Palladian pattern, is indistinguishable from hundreds of others in Bath.

Fig.2 Window Jamb

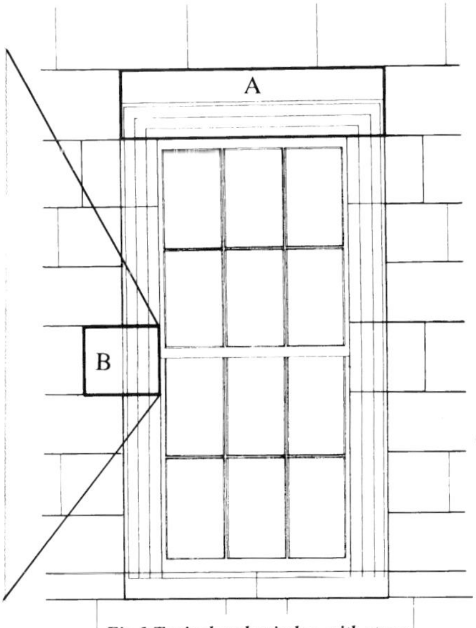

Fig.1 Typical sash window with stone surround

Opposite Page:

Fig.3 Green Street, c1716

Fig.4 Queen Square, c1730

Fig.5 Rivers Street, c1772

Fig.6 Lansdown Crescent, c1790

Fig.7 Belmont, c1770

Fig.8 Brock Street, c1765

Fig.9 Queen Square, c1732

Fig.10 Rivers Street, c1772

Fig.11 Great Pulteney Street, c1790

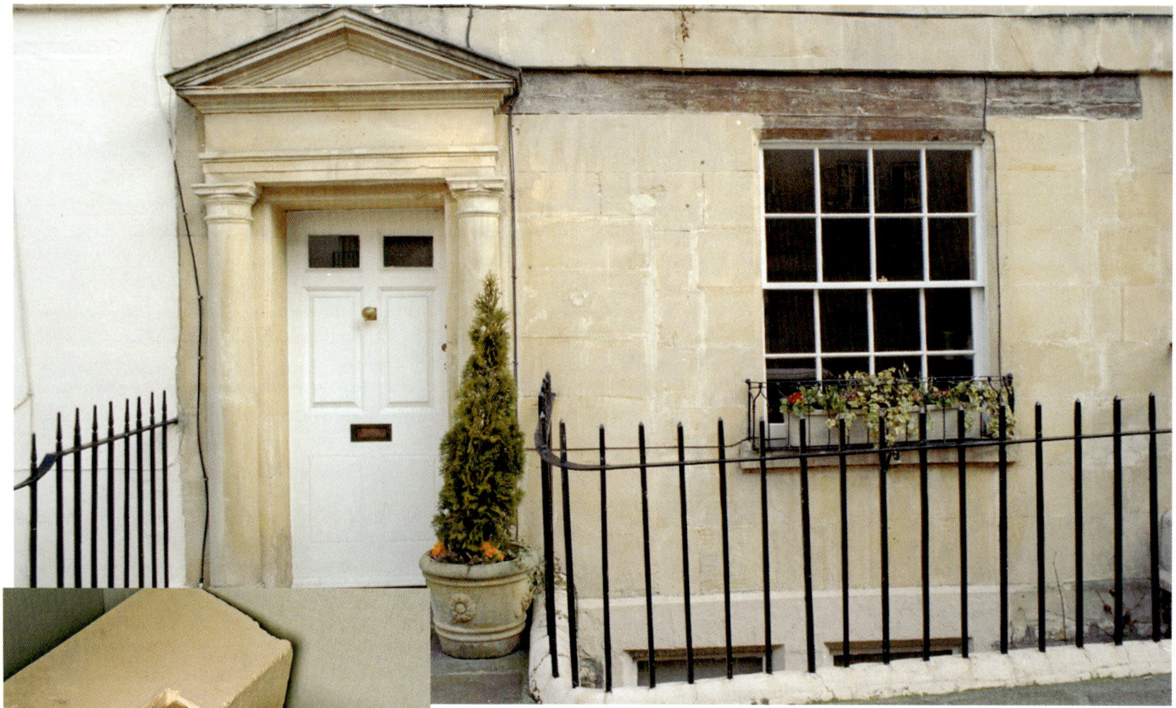

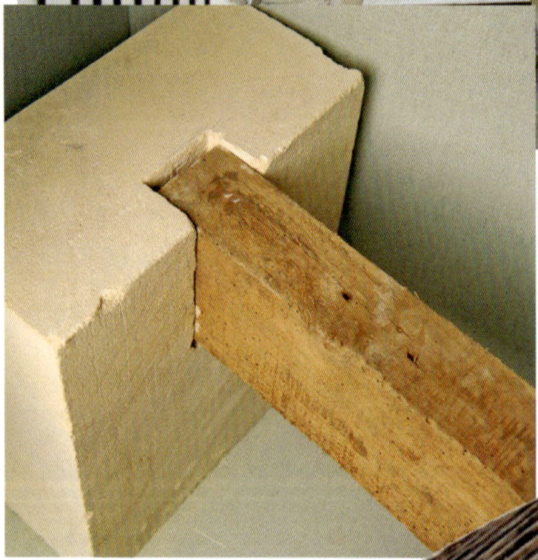

Fig.1 Wooden "bressumer" in Rivers Street

Fig.3 Joist and joist pocket

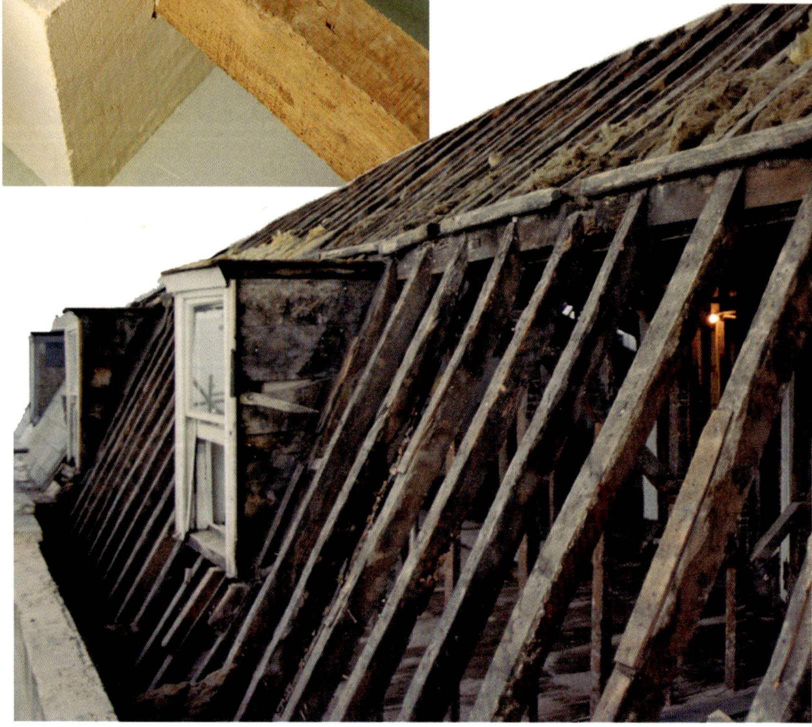

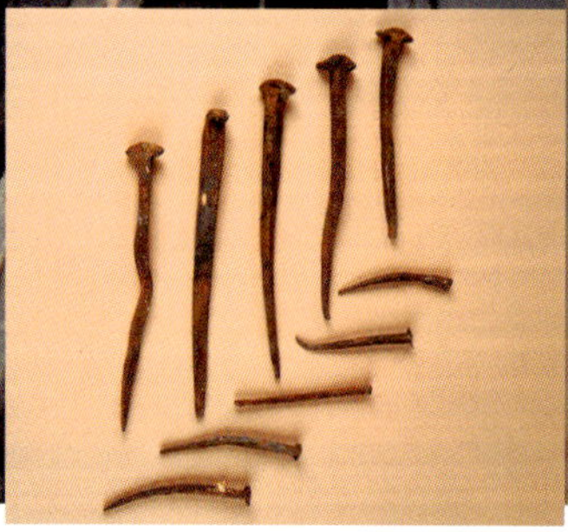

Fig.4 "Mansard" roof at 1 Queen Square

Fig.5 Handcut iron nails, 18th century

CARPENTRY

Carpenters were the most numerous of the tradesmen. They handled all the woodwork in the house that was structural or less delicate in appearance - floors, roofs, timber partitions and so on.

Stout English oak had traditionally been used both for construction and ship building but in the 17th century the combination of the naval wars against the Dutch and the rebuilding of London after the Great Fire led to a crisis in supply. Oak was reserved for the Navy and the construction industry was forced to import sawn lengths of fir - referred to as "deal" - from the Baltic countries.

As soon as the Avon Navigation opened in 1727 imported deal was readily available in Bath. Oak was still preferred if it could be afforded - particularly for important roof timbers - because it was durable and strong and resisted the wet better than deal. However, as deal was much cheaper and easier to prepare and work it was almost always used for structural timbers, floors, doorcases and panelling.

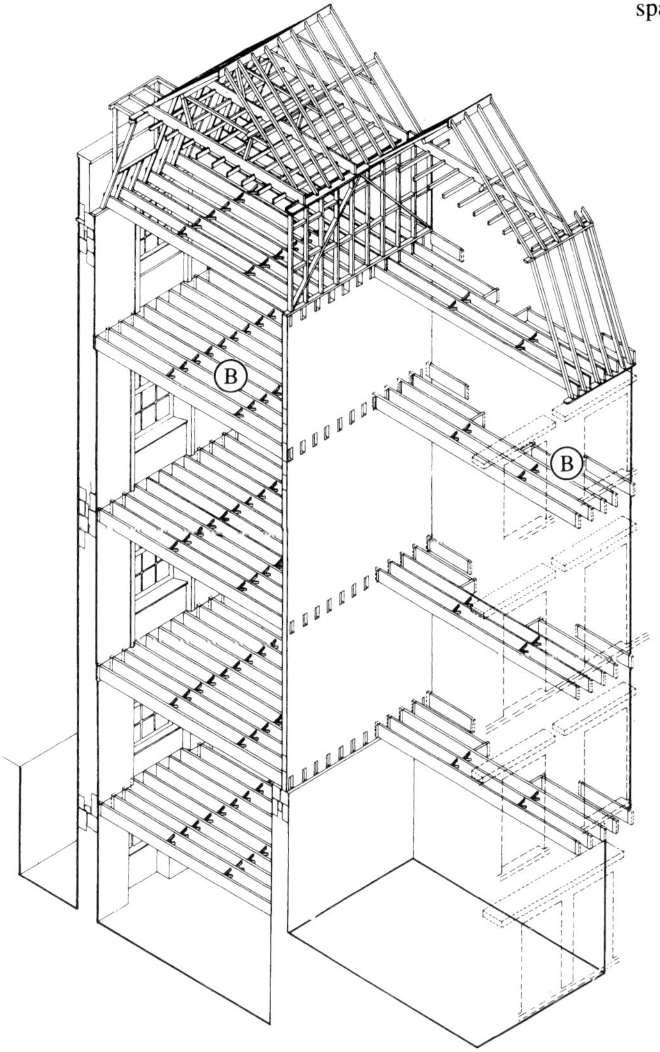

There was a strong fear of fire spreading, and the most important principle of timber construction was that timber should not be exposed on the outside of the building. One exception to this practice was the "bressumer" *(Fig.1)*, a wooden lintel that is often seen above ground floor windows. Its purpose was to absorb the settlement of the wall by spreading the pressure of the masonry above and it also allowed the ground floor to be left open during construction for the builders to carry in bulky materials. The opening was filled in when work neared completion and the bressumer coated with a limewash so that it blended into the stone.

Fig. 2 illustrates the wooden structure of a good Bath house. The floors were supported by wooden beams called "joists" *(Fig. 2b)*. As the joists could not span the full depth of the house they stretched from one external wall to an internal partition wall; each end rested in a pocket in the stone *(Fig. 3)*.

Above the second floor all structural work, apart from the stone party wall, was in timber. In better houses there were servants' rooms in the attic, lit by dormer windows, and to allow space for them the "pitch" - the angle, that is - of the roof changed *(Fig. 4)*. A roof with this profile is known as a "mansard" roof after Francois Mansard, a 17th century French architect who was credited with its invention. Most Bath houses had "double mansards" - two peaks with a valley between them - because it was too difficult to span the full depth of the house with a single timber frame.

The floorboards were sawn and planed down before construction work, and then stacked in a covered shed to season until the roof was finished and the interior therefore protected from the rain. As the floors were partly left bare they were the most visible test of the carpenters' good workmanship. The boards were laid as levelly and precisely as possible and nailed down with hand-cut iron nails *(Fig. 5)*.

One carpenters' trick was to bet an outsider that the latter could not hammer in a nail in a given number of blows. The outsider always lost the wager: each time he struck the nail the hammer would glance off - because one of the carpenters had secretly smeared it with earwax a moment before.

Fig.2 The wooden structure of a typical Bath house

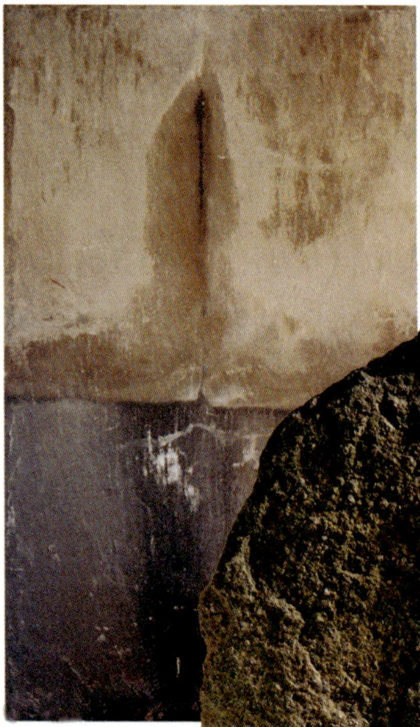

Fig.4 Slate

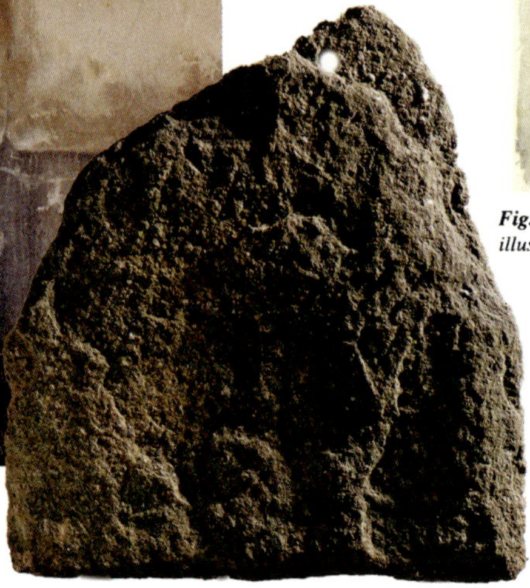

Fig.3 Stone tile

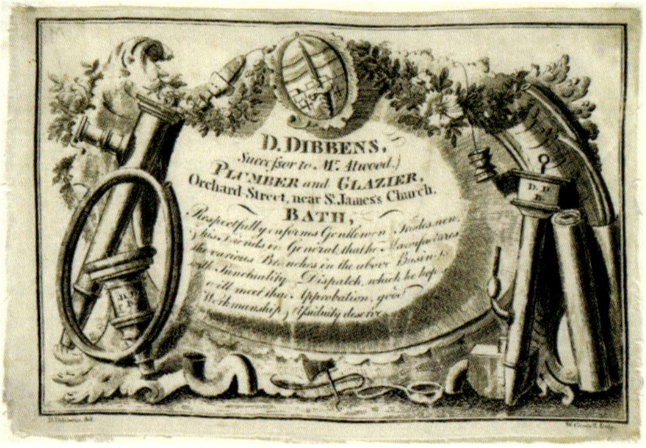

Fig.5 The trade card of Daniel Dibbens, late 18th century, *illustrating the work of a plumber*

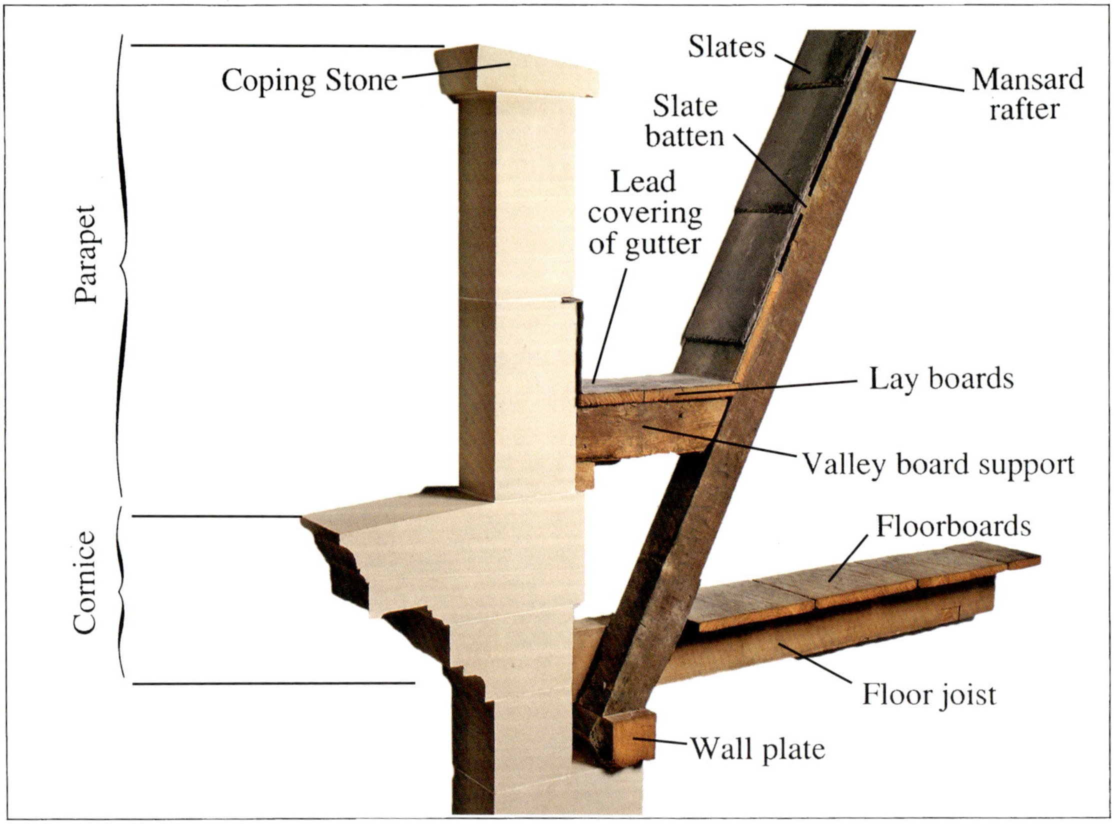

Fig.1 Section through the front of a typical roof

Roof

The roof combined the craftsmanship of carpenters, masons, tilers and plumbers *(Fig. 1)*. The carpenters erected the timber frame - as we have seen - and the tilers nailed wooden battens to the rafters to fix the slates or tiles on to *(Fig. 2a)*.

Until the second half of the 18th century most houses in Bath were roofed with "stone tiles" *(Fig. 3)*, quarried a few miles east of Bath and fixed with oak dowels in overlapping courses. Cornish slate became available once the Avon Navigation opened and, towards the end of the century, Welsh slate also *(Fig. 4)*. Slate is a lighter, durable material and its smooth texture and mathematical regularity suited Georgian taste more than rugged, uneven stone tiles. Over the course of the century slate became the standard material for new houses and eventually it replaced the stone tiles on the older ones. Only a handful of these beautiful stone tile roofs survive in the centre of Bath.

The houses shown on Gilmore's map of 1694 had traditional steep gables to throw off the rain and snow. Palladian architects disliked prominent gables as they distracted attention from their fine facades and as a result nearly all buildings designed after 1720 have low, horizontal rooflines almost concealed by parapets at the front.

The architectural taste of the period had to make some allowances for the English climate. If you look at the stone cornice in *Fig.1*, for example, you will see that its classical profile is set at an angle to throw off the rain, an adjustment that is invisible from the street.

The stone parapet *(Fig. 2b)* had first become a standard feature of Georgian houses in London since the London Building Acts of 1707 outlawed projecting wooden eaves in order to prevent fire spreading from one house to another. This meant that wooden gutters had to be set back behind a stone or brick parapet. Builders in Bath, however, copied the London practice because they wished their houses to be as "modern" as possible. How effectively did a "modern" roof carry out its most important duty, which was, of course, to keep out the rain and snow?

The rain or snow that fell on the front or rear slopes ran down into parapet gutters *(Fig. 2c)* lined with sheets of lead laid on wooden boards. A plumber contracted for all the leadwork *(Fig. 5)* and the surveyor inspected the gutters to check that he had not cheated on the amount.

Draining the concealed roof valley in the centre was even more troublesome. A "secret gutter" *(Fig. 2e)* - also known as a "flying"or "box" gutter - carried the water through the attic to a parapet gutter, normally the one at the rear.

Drainpipes made of lead *(Fig. 2d)* - though stone or wooden pipes were common at the beginning of our period and iron ones at the end - carried the water from the parapet gutters down to the basement. Several houses might share a single pipe at the front to avoid cluttering up the facades. On the better streets the pipes were either concealed inside the front wall - as on Royal Crescent, for example - or there was a secret gutter to carry all the water in the front parapet gutter right through the attic to the drainpipes 'at the rear. The rainwater then ran through narrow ashlar drains into the Grand Common Sewer under the street *(see page 15)*, although a wooden barrel or lead cistern often stood in the basement to collect a quantity for the household's use.

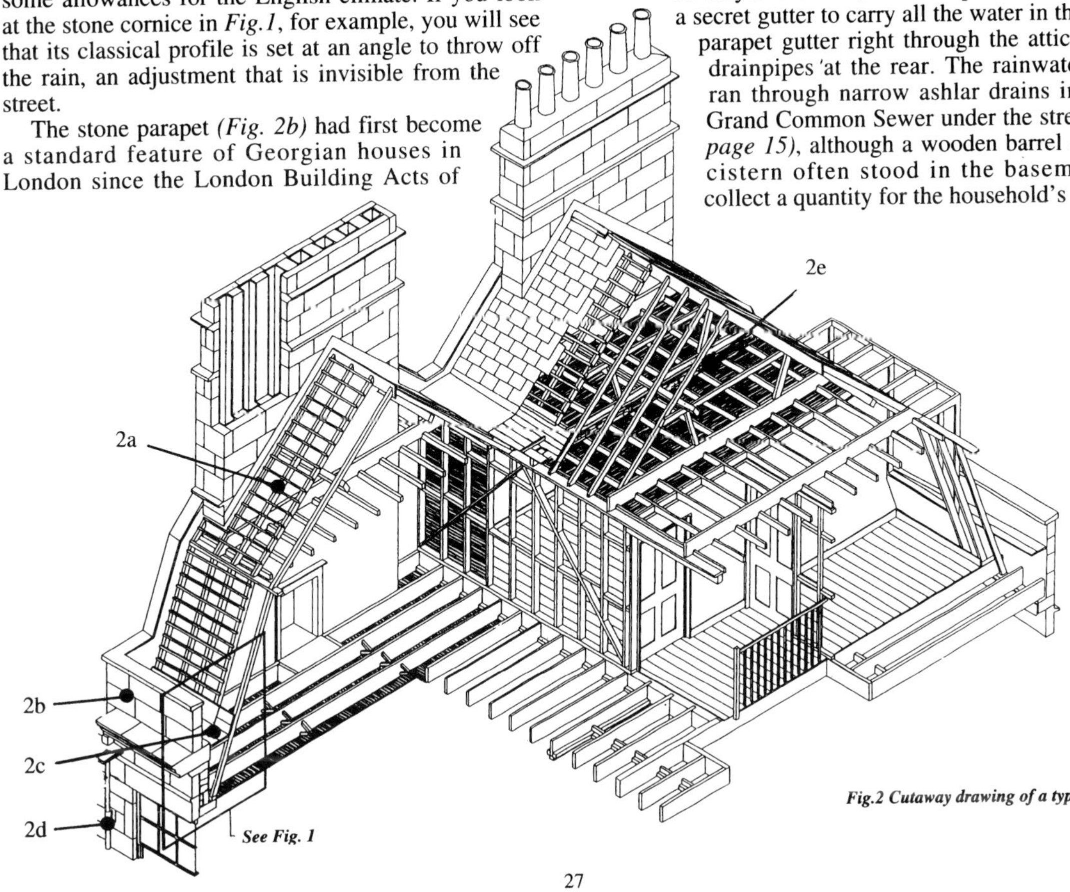

Fig.2 Cutaway drawing of a typical roof

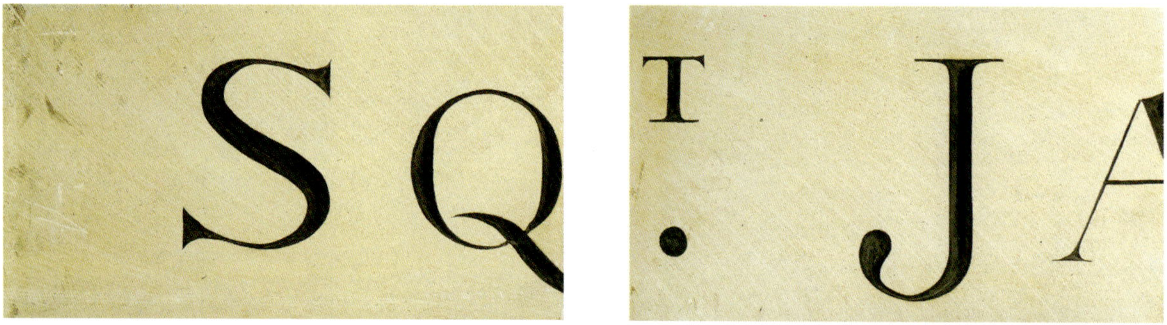

Fig.1 Carved and painted street lettering

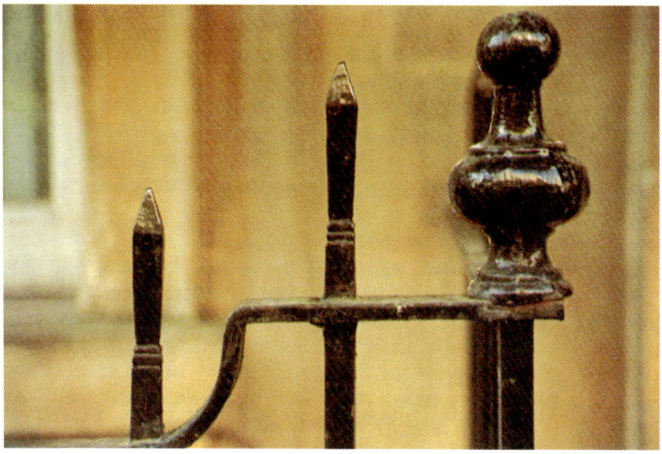

Fig.2 Wrought iron railings and urn at North Parade Buildings, c1750

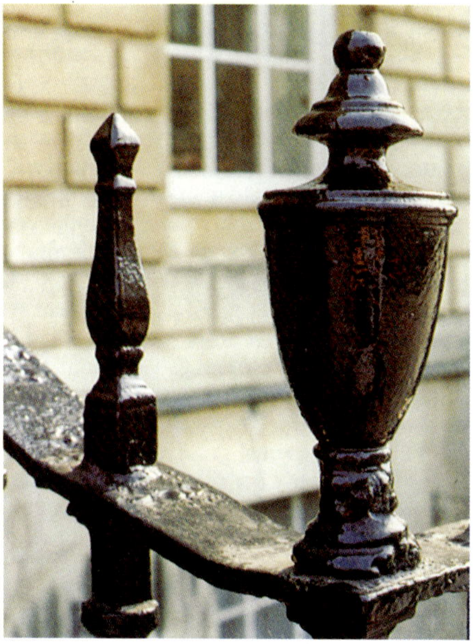

Fig.4 Cast iron urn in Great Pulteney Street, c1790

Fig.5 Pitching and paving on Royal Cresent

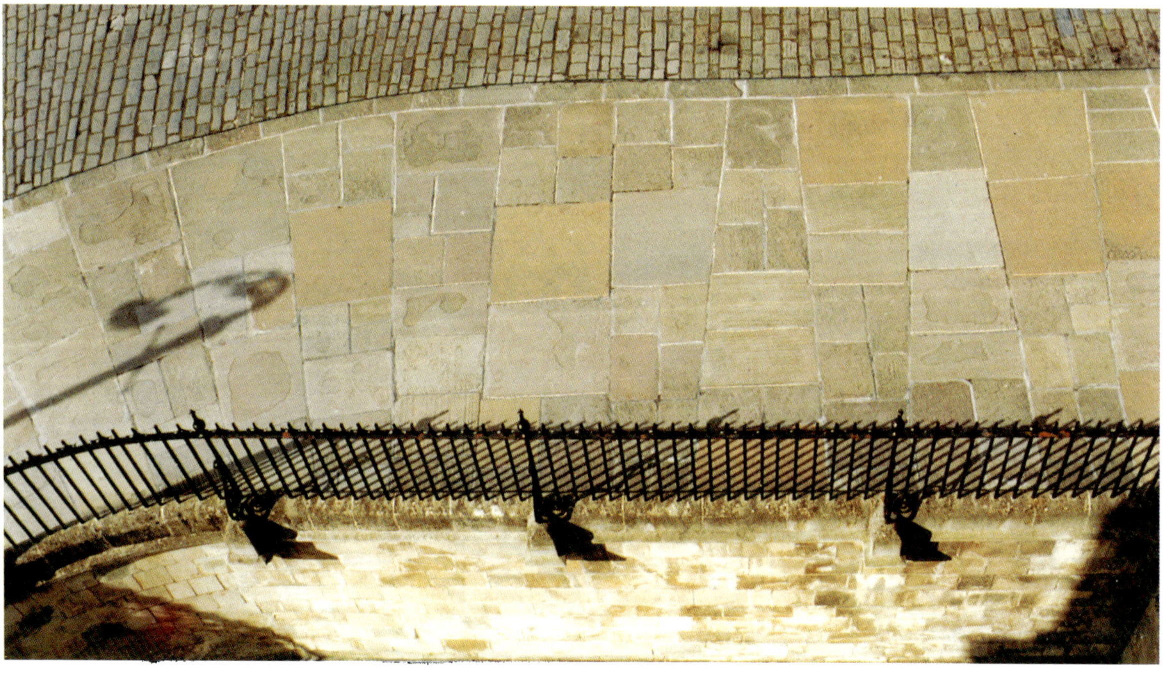

THE STREET

In the 17th century open drains ran down the street to carry away the rainwater and John Wood wrote, in his *Description of Bath* (1765) how *"the streets and public ways of the City were become like so many dunghills, slaughterhouses and pigsties: for soil of all sorts and even carrion were cast and laid in the streets..."*

The condition of the streets and pavements improved, however, as the resort became more polite and sophisticated in character. In 1707 the City Corporation implemented the first in a series of "Improvement Acts" for paving, lighting and cleansing the streets.

The number of street names dating from the late Georgian period is one sign of this growing orderliness. The letters were either painted straight on to a wall or, as in *Fig.1*, carved into the stone and then painted.

A screen of iron railings was erected in front of every house that had a basement area, to stop anyone falling in and to deter intruders. For most of our period these railings were of "wrought iron" (*Fig. 2*).

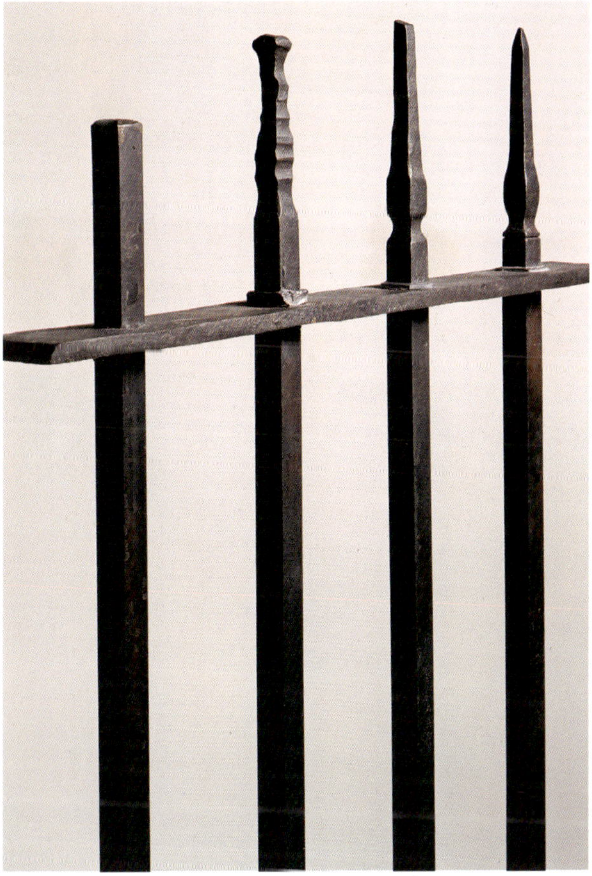

A blacksmith in Bath purchased iron bars of standard lengths imported from the furnaces and forges of the Forest of Dean and other iron producing areas as far afield as Sweden and Russia. These he could reheat and hammer into shape in his forge. The upright bars and flat horizontal rails of the railings were plainly finished but the blacksmith worked the sharp tips of the railings - called "finials" - into decorative patterns. *Fig. 3* illustrates four stages in this process.

"Cast iron", made by pouring molten iron into sand moulds, was cheaper as it called for less labour but it was too brittle to be used for railings. Casting methods improved at the very end of the 18th century and there are some decorative cast iron fixtures in Bath, for example the urn in *Fig. 4*. You can often tell cast iron apart from hammered iron by its delicate lines and smoother finish.

Nowadays all ironwork is painted a familiar, monotonous black but in the Georgian period you would see it painted bright blue, grey, "stone colour" and dark green as well. Some historians say that railings were only painted a uniform black as a mark of mourning when Prince Albert died in 1861.

The visiting "company" spent many hours promenading around Bath, and the broad and even pavements were one of the city's principal attractions. Visitors accustomed to the rough, unpaved roadways of other provincial towns were most impressed. Developers obliged builders to lay a pavement in front of the house and "pitch" - that is, pave with smaller stones laid on their sides - the roadway up to the middle of the street.

Bath stone was used for pitching and paving in the early decades of the century but it was too soft to resist the frost or stand up to the constant pounding of traffic. Also, horses' hooves and carriage wheels threw up clouds of stone dust which was churned into a mire when it rained, obliging ladies to wear platformed shoes called "pattens". In its place, a hard sandstone called "pennant" was imported from quarries near Bristol for the pavements, kerbs and steps *(Fig. 5)*. The roadway was laid with blocks of pennant or "blue lias", quarried to the west of the city. These stones are extremely hard and although it was immensely tough work to dress them into shape they have endured to this day.

Fig.3 Wrought iron railings showing four stages in the work of the smith

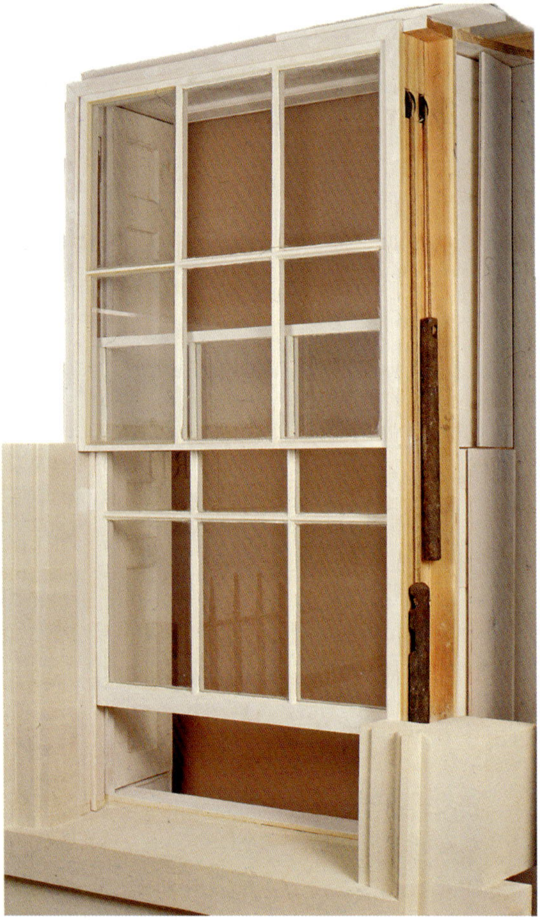

Fig.1 Sash window, exterior

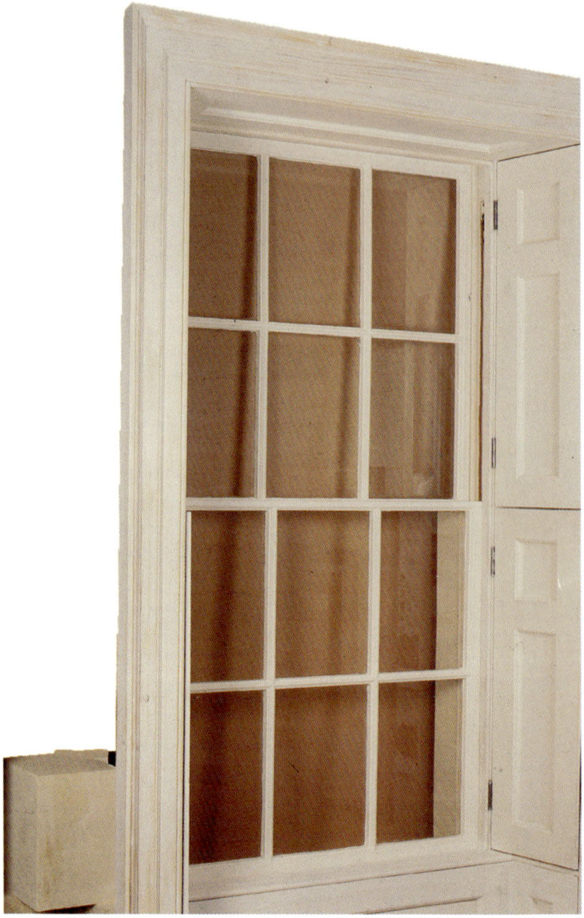

Fig.2 Sash window, interior

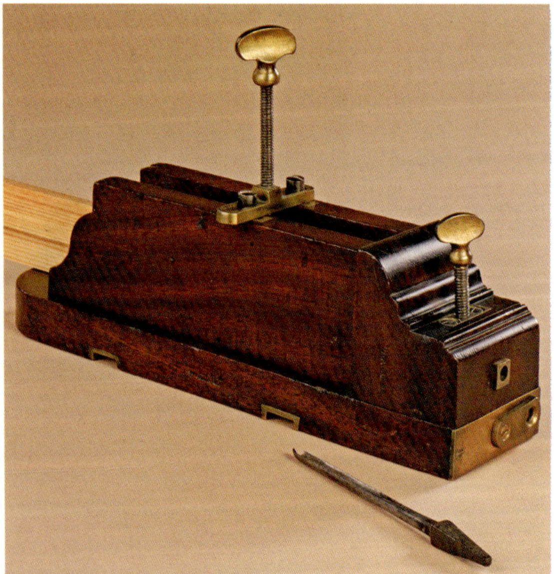

Fig.5 Sash dowelling box and metal bit, c1790

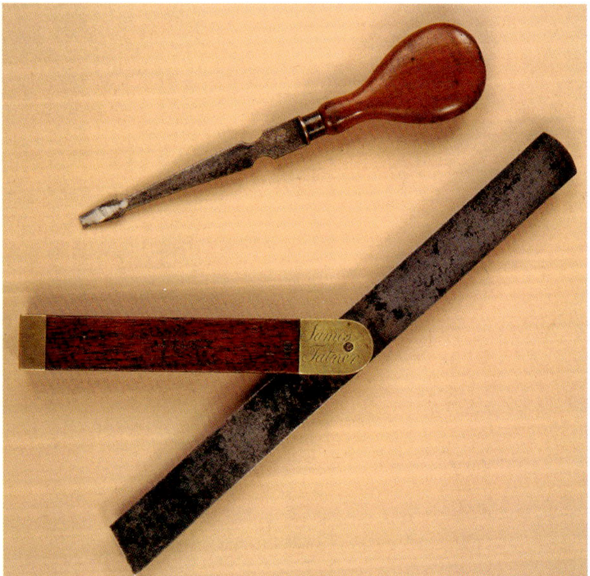

Fig.6 Bevel; mahogany, brass and steel, c1800 (bottom)
Fig.7 "Turnscrew"; with mahogany handle (top)

The Sash Window

A row of neat sash windows is one of the most familiar features of a Georgian house. The sash window drew together the technology of fine joinery, glazing, putty and oil painting.

Figs. 1 and *2* show a replica of a double hung sash window from the ground floor of a typical Bath house of 1765, with sections cut away to give you a better insight. As to why it is called a sash window, the name probably derives from the French word *chassis*, meaning frame.

Sash windows were first used in Britain in the 1670s and were introduced to Bath by 1694. They were the sign of a modern, comfortable house and by the 1720s most good new houses in Bath were "sashed". They were also installed on older houses, replacing "casement" windows - which swing open sideways on hinges - or fixed windows which you could not open at all. As John Wood wrote: *"...low and obscure lights were turned into elegant sash windows"*. The practical advantage of the new sash window was that it was simple to use, kept out draughts and could be left open at any height you desired.

Let us now take a closer look at the outside of the window *(Fig. 1)*. The two wooden frames - the "sashes", that is - are set back behind the stone surround and the bottom one sits on a stone window sill. In other parts of the country the sills were made of wood, but Bath stone could be cut so accurately that it was standard local practice to dispense with the wooden sill.

The sashes slide up or down and if you release one at the height you require it will hang in that position. How does this simple but effective mechanism work? As you slide the sash up metal weights descend at either side inside in a wooden "sash box". The weights and the sash are both suspended from the same cords, leading over a small pulley wheel. The two weights - always of lead until cast iron was introduced in the late 18th century - add up to the same weight as the sash so they balance each other in mid-air. As the sash hung from the cords it was not subjected to any bending stress so its construction could be very light.

Each sash is an exact square in proportion and divided into six panes. From the middle of the 18th century to the middle of the 19th century, when sheet glass became widely available *(see page 23)*, windows were glazed with smaller panes of "crown glass", installed by a glazier using putty.

Bath's crown glass was probably manufactured in Bristol. At the glass furnace molten glass was blown into a globe *(Fig. 3)*. The globe was then attached to an iron rod and spun at some speed until it spread out into a circular disc *(Fig. 4)* called a "table". The panes of "crown glass" were cut from these "tables", between three and five feet in diameter. This method of manufacture was the reason for the limited size of the panes and their sparkling, wavy surface, on which sunlight ripples with such liveliness. And why is it called "crown glass"? It was first manufactured in England at the Duke of Buckingham's works at Southwark in 1672 and the centre of each table was stamped with his ducal coronet.

The size of the panes made wooden glazing bars necessary. Those in our example are moulded with a decorative profile called an "astragal and hollow" and are 7/8" wide.

Special hand tools were developed to speed the work of making a sash window, for example, the "sash dowelling box" and "bit" *(Figs. 5a & 5b)*. More general tools *(Fig. 6)* such as a bevel and, for the iron fittings, a "turnscrew" - the old name for a screwdriver - would also be necessary. In Bath there are still some sashes - usually on the backs of houses because of the mania for installing sheet glass at the front - that are original and are now over 200 years old.

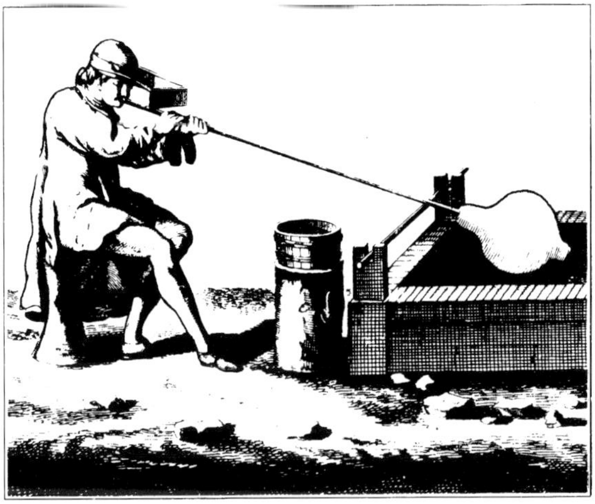

Fig.3 Crown glass manufacture: blowing glass into a globe
from L'Encyclopédie Diderot, Paris 1762 - 77

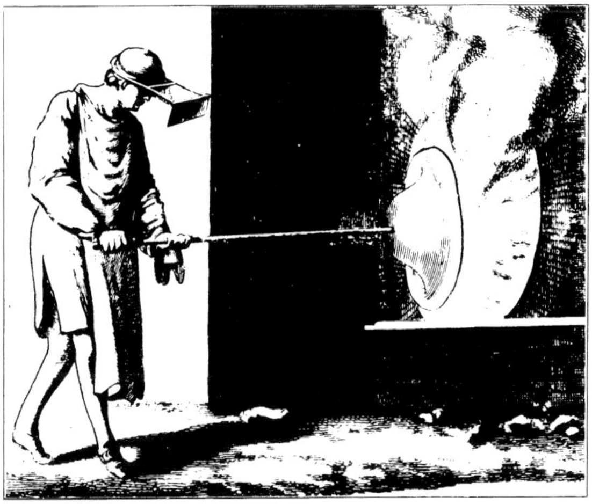

Fig.4 Crown glass manufacture: spinning the "table"
from L'Encyclopédie Diderot, Paris 1762 - 77

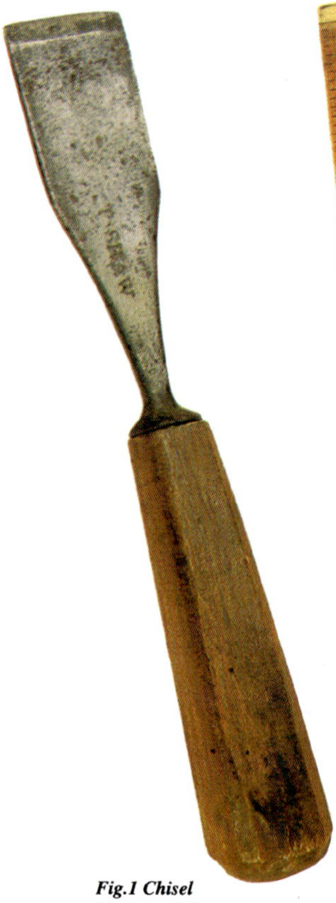

Fig.1 Chisel
Made by T.Shaw of Sheffield, c1790

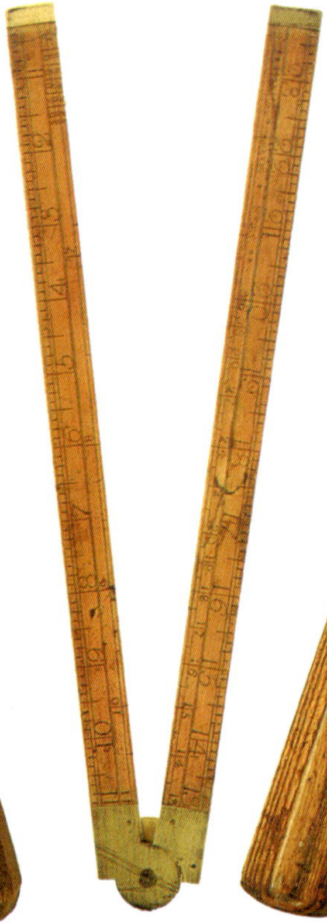

Fig.2 Measuring rule, boxwood and brass;
made by T.Webb of Bristol, c1800

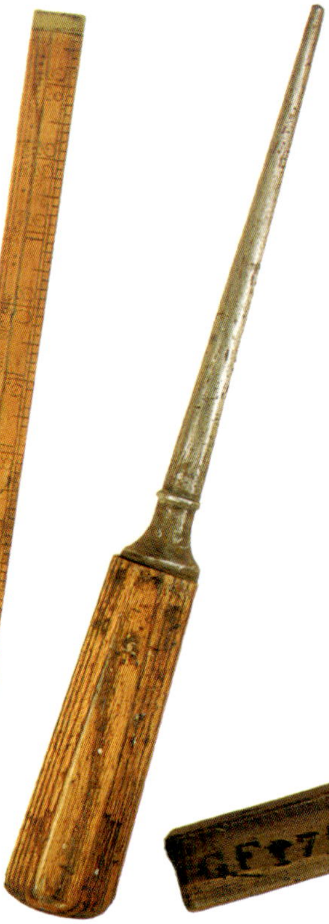

Fig.3 Drawbore pin, c1800

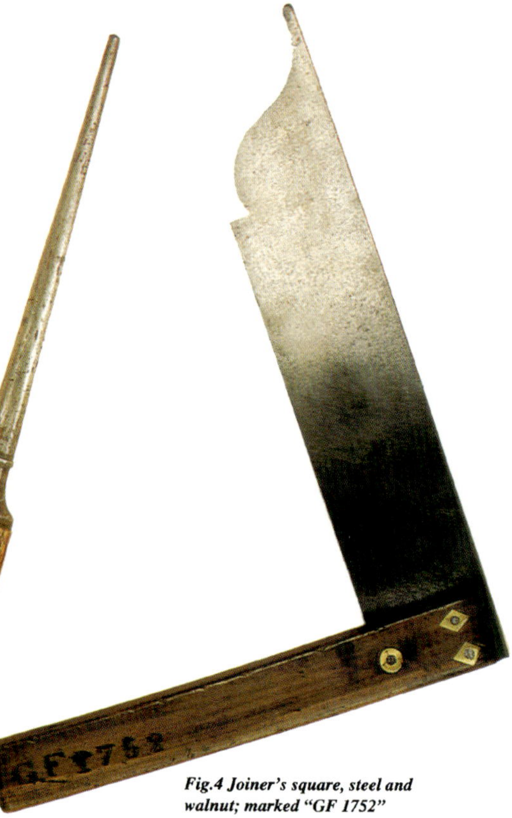

Fig.4 Joiner's square, steel and walnut; marked "GF 1752"

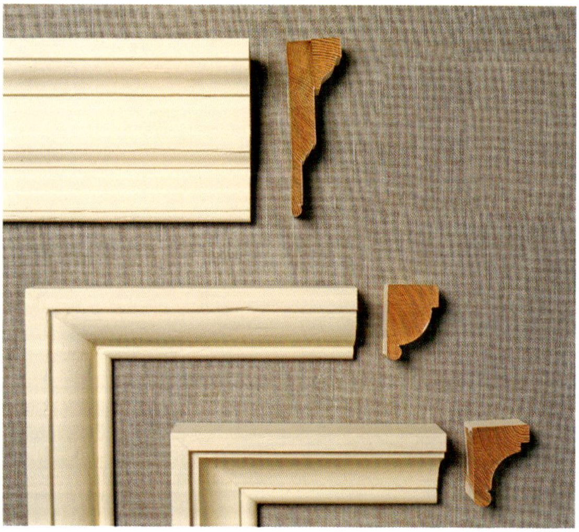

***Fig.6 Some examples of wooden mouldings** made by a joiner*

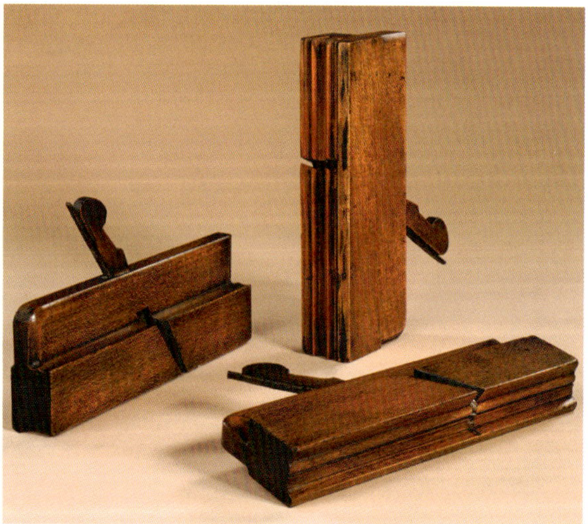

***Fig.7 Moulding planes** from the Harding family's workshop*

JOINERY

As you stand inside the window you face the wooden panelling and the shutters, folded back against the wall. Wooden panelling, shutters, the window itself, doors, doorcases, cupboards and mouldings were the work of a "joiner".

Few of the joiner's tools have changed since the 18th century and some of the most essential ones are illustrated: a chisel *(Fig. 1)*, a measuring rule *(Fig. 2)*, a drawbore pin *(Fig. 3)* - for pulling mortice or tenon joints up tight - and a square *(Fig. 4)*. One past owner has carved "G F 1752" - his initials and the date - in the walnut stock of the square to prevent it being stolen. Even in the 18th century many tools were being made by commercial makers and they also stamped their names on tools.

In the 17th century woods such as cedar, oak and walnut were favoured for internal joinery. These were of good appearance and left unpainted. In the Georgian period, however, "deal" was used for the sake of economy for all internal joinery and, because of its poorer appearance, it was always painted. The quality of joinery depended on the class of house and the importance of the particular room. For example, there would be fine panelling and ornate mouldings on the fine first floor rooms and plainer work in the bedrooms on the floor above.

The interiors of all but the plainest rooms would have their heights divided up to correspond to the parts of a classical column *(Fig. 5a and Fig. 5b)*, as was also done with the facade. At the beginning of our period the full height of the room would be panelled in wainscot. Around the middle of the century, however, it became standard practice to plaster between the dado and the cornice.

All but the poorest 18th century houses were built with wooden "mouldings" for the skirting, dado, cornice, doorcases and window surrounds. "Mouldings" are profiled wooden sections and making and fitting them was the task of a joiner. Mouldings were not only decorative: they were also used to conceal joints or gaps between different materials.

Fig. 6 illustrates some examples of doorcase mouldings, each with a different profile. More ornate mouldings - for example, *Fig 6a* - were formed by fixing different pieces together. The joiner's art was such that when these are seen from the usual point of view - not in section, that is - they appear as a single piece of wood.

Mouldings were made using "moulding planes" *(Fig. 7)* - at some speed. The "iron" - the blade - and the wooden "sole" of each plane had a different profile. There would be a large stock of moulding planes in the workshop; those on display in the Museum are a small part of one family workshop's collection of no less than 170 planes dating back to the building of Georgian Bath.

The joiner chose the design for the moulding from the familiar stock at his fingertips or by adapting the classical shapes in pattern books to his own purposes. These designs changed over the years with the various architectural fashions.

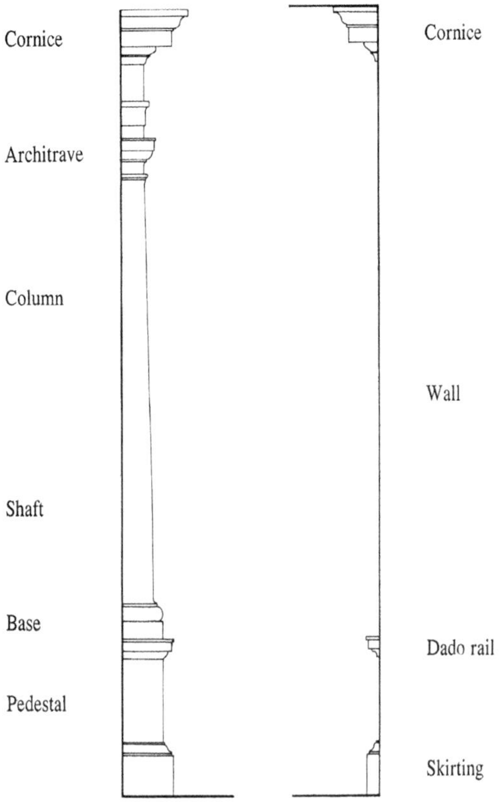

Fig.5 Diagram showing relationship between (a) a classical column and (b) a domestic interior of the 18th century

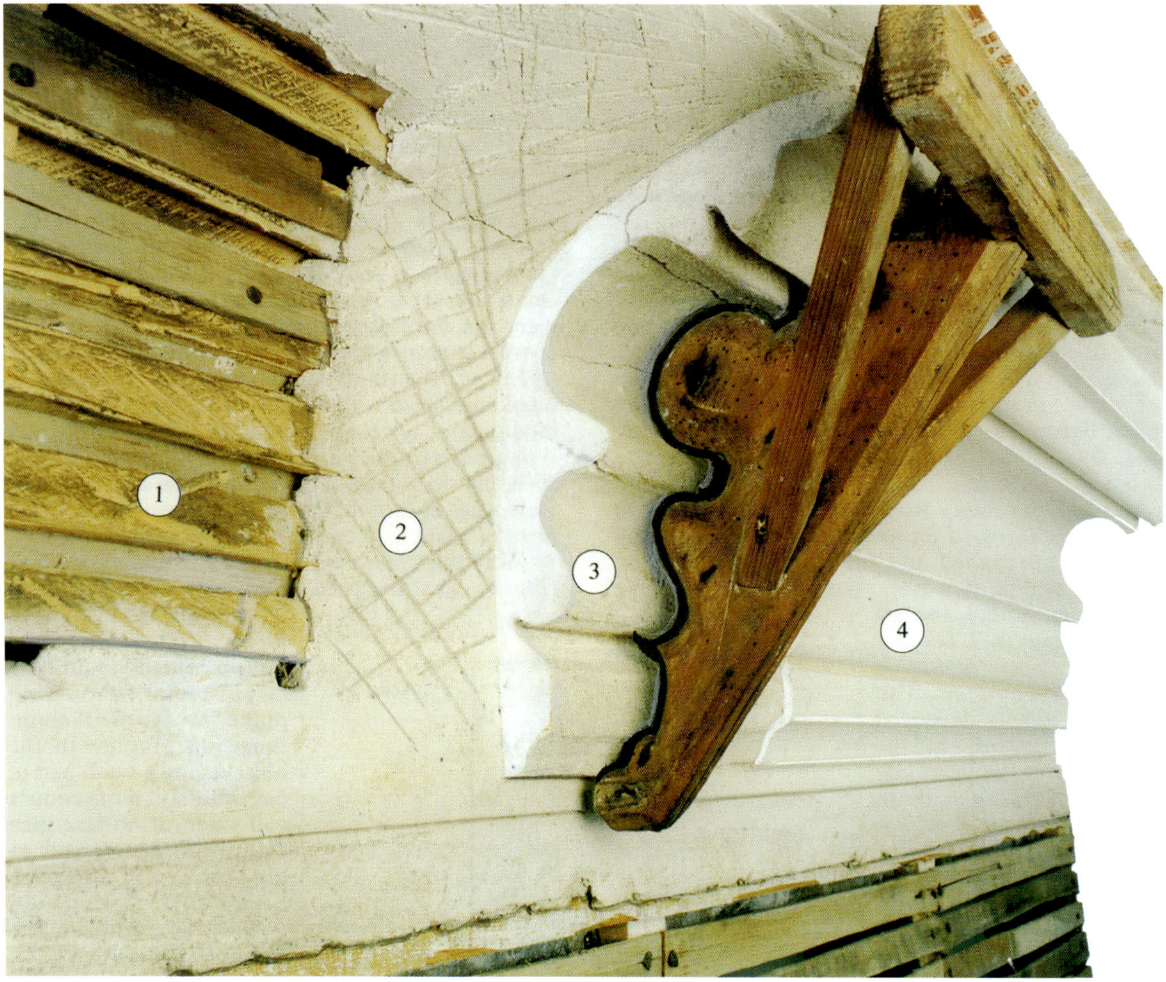

Fig.2 Mock-up of partition wall and cornice being plastered, in the manner of the early 19th century

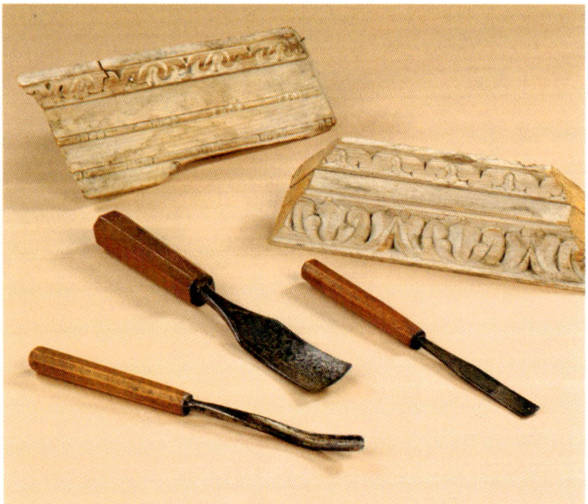

Fig.1 Fragments of enriched wooden mouldings with carver's chisel and gouges

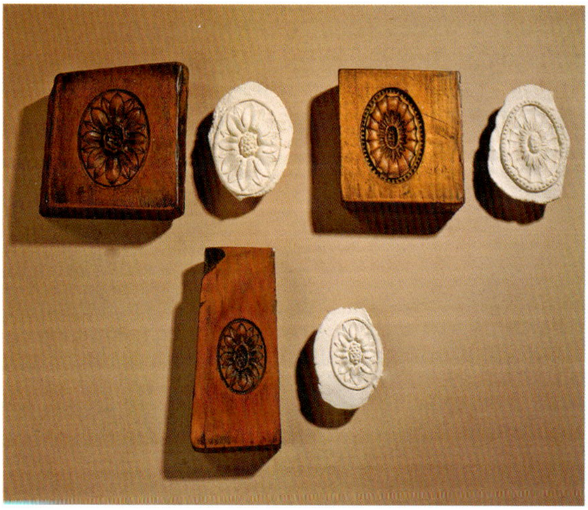

Fig.4 Boxwood "compo" moulds from the late 18th century with their "compo" products, before trimming

Ornamentation

More ornate and fanciful wooden decorations were the work of a "carver". Carving was a separate trade to joinery, with its own special tools such as the chisel and gouges in *Fig. 1*. Enriching mouldings, as in *Fig. 1*, was one skill. Carvers also made rich classical ornaments, such as capitals or festoons, and used forms taken from nature, like leaves, foliage and birds.

These carved enrichments were expensive, however, and are only occasionally seen in the Georgian houses of Bath. Indeed, a disappointingly small number of interiors in houses in Georgian Bath have lavish interiors, because nearly all of them were built as speculations. The occupiers purchased houses from speculating builders as bare shells and if they wanted to improve the interior they had to pay for the extra work themselves. A high proportion were lodging-house keepers who had no interest in spending more than was necessary to give their seasonal visitors a comfortable stay.

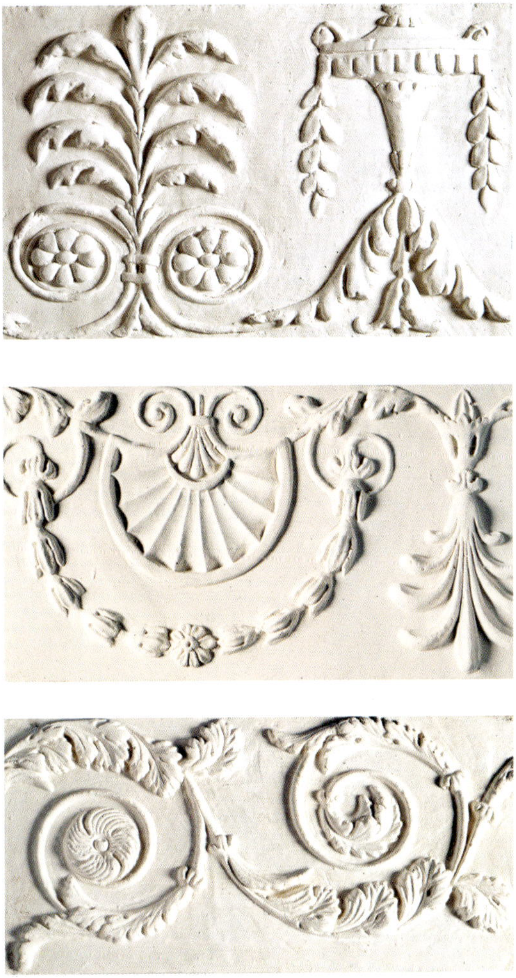

Fig.3 Decorative plasterwork from various Bath houses, late 18th century

The finest interiors in Georgian Bath were paid for by clients who intended to take up residence there for some time. One frequent exception to this rule occurs where a house was built as a plasterer's speculation. It is quite likely to have fine plasterwork as it was an opportunity for him to raise the selling price of the house and display his skill at the same time.

Around the middle of the 18th century plaster cornices began to replace wooden ones and internal walls came to be plastered, not panelled, above the dado rail. Plaster was quicker and cheaper to apply and better suited to the slender and delicate ornaments that were coming into fashion.

The different stages in plastering a wall and cornice are shown in *Fig. 2*. The carpenter would have already erected the partition walls, using poor quality timber, and the first stage in the plasterer's work would be the tedious task - which he passed on to an apprentice - of nailing on rough strips of wood called "laths". The plasterer stood on a scaffold or planks laid on trestles and applied a rough coat of plaster to the laths, with coarse cattle hair mixed in to bind it together. Plaster was made from lime, sand and water. The first coat was scratched to "key in" with further layers of a smoother plaster, made with burnt gypsum in place of the lime. The plasterer built up the cornice in this way and created its profile by running a wooden template with a metal edge over the wet plaster.

The template in *Fig. 2* has quite a bold and projecting profile. Most cornices in our period were flatter in profile and these could easily be enlivened by applying pieces of decorative plaster *(Fig. 3)*. Panels and enrichments - these examples are in the light and graceful style popular in the late 18th century - were cast by pouring plaster into wood or wax moulds. Each plasterer's workshop would possess a stock of moulds in a variety of designs. Plasterers, like the other tradesmen decorating the interior, rarely worked to the directions of an architect or surveyor. They were all trying to make a good living, however, and followed the latest architectural fashions as closely as they could.

"Composition" is a harder material, used for ornaments on mirror frames, chimneypieces, furniture and in other positions where plaster would get broken. It was made by combining "whiting" (ground chalk), rabbit glue, resin and linseed oil, in a container immersed in hot water. The putty-like mixture was then pressed into moulds while it was still warm and immediately pulled out *(Fig. 4)*, trimmed and, while still flexible, applied to the chosen background. It would then have been either painted or gilded. These exquisite "compo" moulds were reverse carved out of boxwood, a very hard, fine-grained wood.

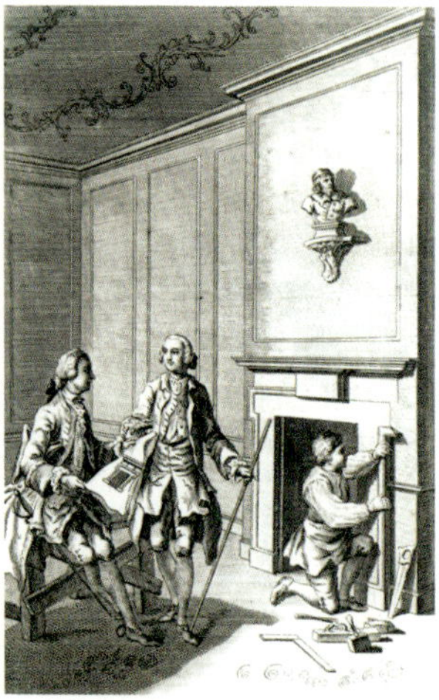

l Fitting up the fireplace, 1766
page from Crunden's Chimneypiece er's Daily Assistant - Reproduced by tesy of the Board of Trustees of the ria and Albert Museum

Fig.4 Wallpaper - *from St James's Square. Early 19th century.*

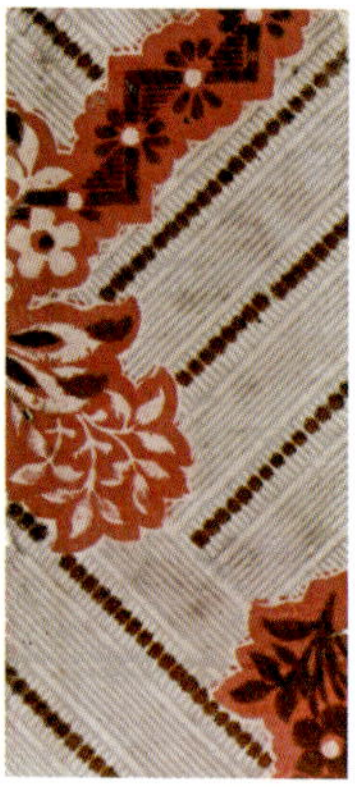

Fig.5 "Flock" Wallpaper - *from a house adjoining The Circus. Possibly 1765/ 1770.*

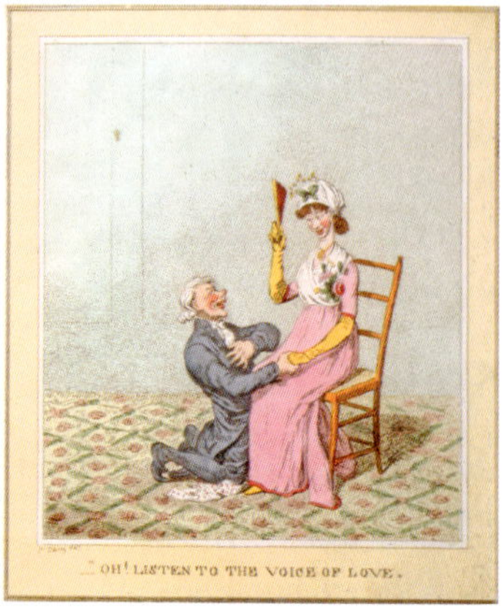

Fig.8 Coloured engraving *"Oh listen to the voice of love" showing repeat pattern woven carpet.*

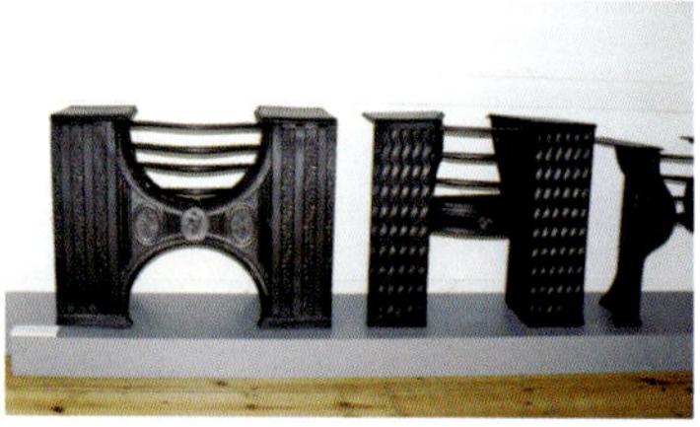

2 Three cast iron hob-grates, from houses in ı c.1775 - c.1820 *- made at Coalbrookdale, pshire and the Carron Foundry, Scotland. Kindly by Roman Baths Museum*

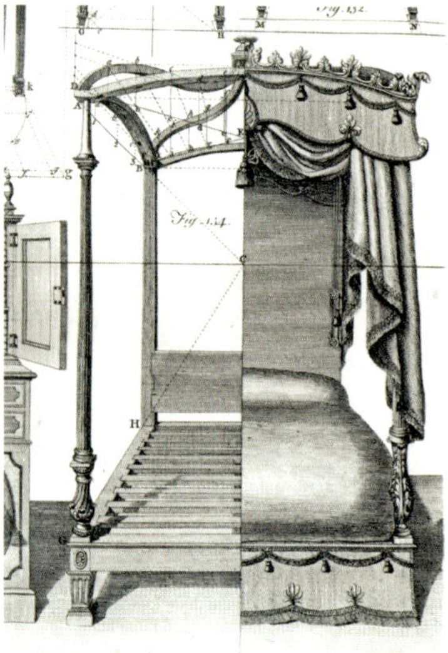

Fig.6 Engraving of a bed showing its construction *- From Thomas Malton's Treatise on Perspective, 1775*

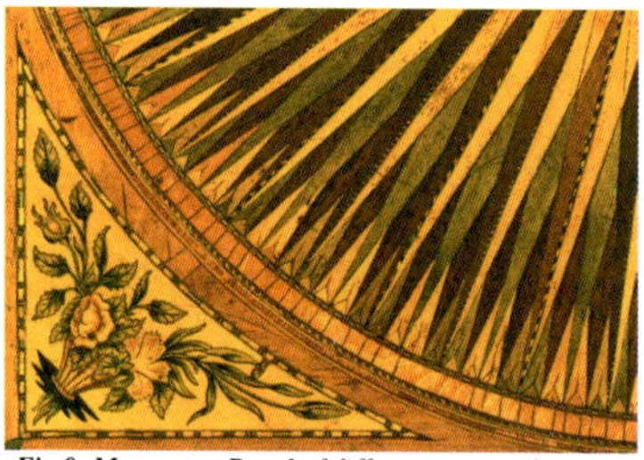

Fig.9 Marquetry Panel *of different veneers for decorating cabinet work*

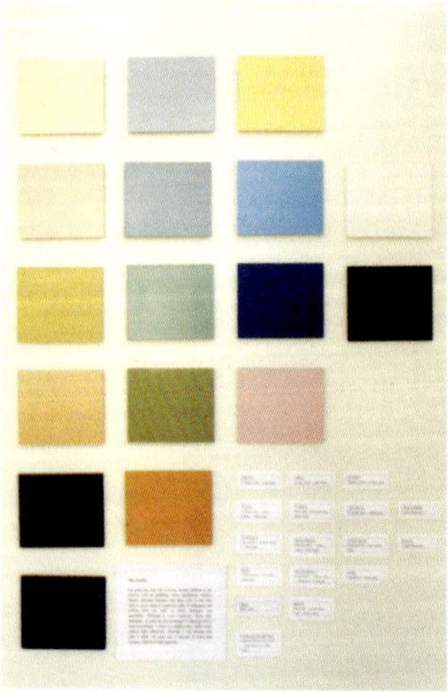

3 Panel showing different coloured oil ıts based on 18th century paint cipes"

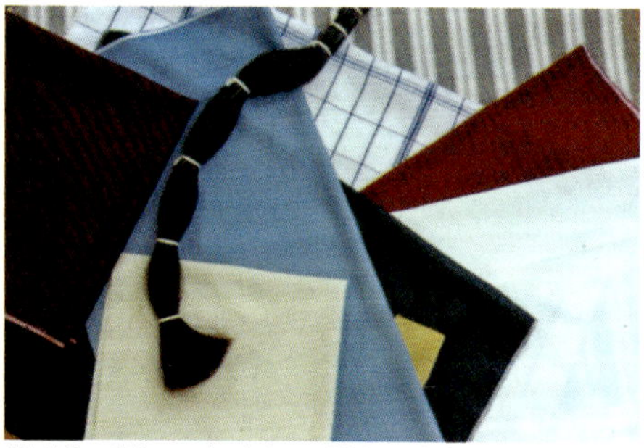

Fig.7 Furnishing and upholstery fabrics *including, moreen, camlet, flannel, tammy, Manchester linen check and a horse's tail for weaving into cloth*

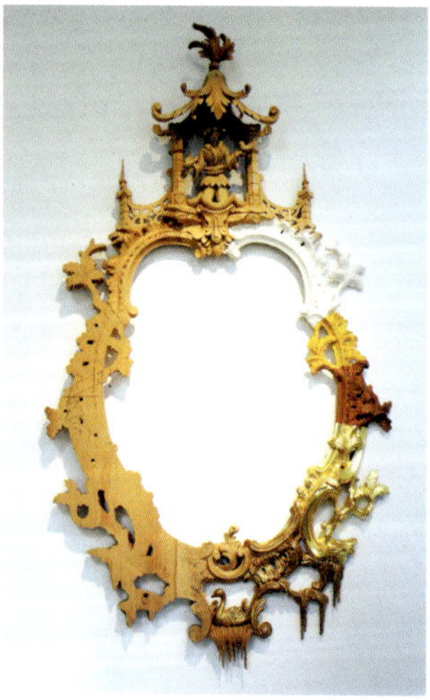

Fig. 10 Frame carved in pine, *showing stages of the carving and gilding process.*

The Interior

When the walls of the house were plastered and dry, many different specialist craftsmen would come to decorate and furnish the interior. Among the first to begin would be the mason or joiner who would fit the chimneypieces and grates (Fig 1). Chimneypieces for the finest rooms were generally made of marble and could be highly carved and decorated. Many beautiful Italian marbles were imported into Bath through the port of Bristol. Other chimneypieces were made of wood or local stone. Early in the period the fireplace might be fitted with a basket grate but from the 1760's the most popular type was the iron hob-grate (Fig 2). These were mass produced at Coalbrookdale in Shropshire and by the Carron Foundry in Scotland. Various standard sizes were made to fit elegant drawing rooms, bedchambers and tiny attics in Bath. Coal from North Somerset was burnt in the grates, often causing serious air pollution in the City.

The house painter would distemper or paint walls, ceilings and interior woodwork. He charged for the area he covered; 50 to 60 square yards was regarded as a good day's work. He used a reasonably wide range of colours, from ones prepared with rare and expensive imported pigments (malachite or lapis lazuli) to cheaper or "common" colours prepared from local materials such as ochres found in deposits near Bristol and Bath. (Fig 3).

Oil paints were used to cover woodwork: they were mixed from white lead, linseed oil and pigment. Preparing oil paints was a hazard to health, and some 'colour-men' are known to have come to Bath to seek a cure from lead-poisoning. Distempers were used on ceilings and the walls of lesser rooms. These were water-based mixtures using whiting (ground chalk) pigments and size, a form of glue made from boiled animal skin and bones – often rabbit.

Bath house-painters might mix their own colours or retail ready-mixed paint, and sometimes combined this business with glazing, sign writing and print selling.

Wallpapers became increasingly popular during the Georgian period , especially for sitting rooms and bedrooms (Fig.4). Wallpapers were not manufactured in Bath but the city's upholsterers and paint sellers stocked the latest patterns made in London. The papers were made from pulped rags, painted with a background colour and then hand printed with patterns carved on wooden blocks. Sometimes up to fifteen blocks might be used to create one pattern. "Flock" (Fig5) papers were made by printing glue onto the paper and scattering wool shavings over the sticky surface to create an imitation of velvet. As a luxury item, wallpapers were taxed from 1712 onwards and had to be stamped by inspectors before sale.

The upholsterer or upholder was the craftsman responsible for providing soft furnishings and might also advise on an overall scheme of decoration in the manner of the modern interior decorator. He could provide window curtains and blinds, bed hangings and mattresses (Fig 6), upholstered chairs and carpets. Many of Bath's upholsterers, such as John Bryant in the 1760's, ran huge businesses and offered to furnish a house completely within a very few days. He offered furniture and sedan chairs for hire for shorter term visitors and like others ran an undertaking service for those who were not cured by the medical treatments of Bath and died in the city.

Furnishing materials came to Bath from all over Britain and beyond, and were sold by mercers. Worsted woollens from Norwich were particularly popular for winter bed hangings. They had many different names such as harrateen, moreen, camlet and calimanco. Printed cottons came from the developing industries of North West England for summer hangings. Woven horsehair (made from horses' tails) was used to cover parlour, dining and library chairs as it was very durable and easy to clean. Curled horsehair was used to stuff chair seats. (Fig 7).

Carpets were used extensively in Georgian houses. The finest were imported Persian, Turkish or French ones, but machine woven strips were sewn together to provide relatively cheap wall-to-wall carpets. They are recognisable by their simple repeating patterns (Fig 8).

Bath's cabinet makers supplied furniture for all the different rooms of the house, including desks, chests of drawers, tables, cupboards and sideboards. Fashionable pieces were often made from mahogany imported from the West Indies through Bristol. Many other attractive and exotic woods were used in veneers (thin slices of timber) to decorate the surfaces of cabinet work (Fig 9).

Carvers and gilders produced mirror and picture frames, carved chimneypieces and chair frames. The most decorative pieces took a long time and great skill to carve before being passed to the specialist gilder. He would apply thin layers of gold leaf to the prepared wood to provide a beautiful reflective finish. Mirror glass was extremely expensive and was often recycled when broken or worn. (Fig 10).

These were the principle craftsmen who would help fit up a house for inhabitation, but many others were also involved, including locksmiths, braziers, tin-smiths, joiners, wax and tallow-chandlers. Between them, many of Bath's Georgian houses were very elegantly decorated and furnished and kept in good repair.

LIFE IN A GEORGIAN HOUSE

The house in this cross-section is at present - 1765, that is - occupied by George Wicksteed Esq. and Mrs Wicksteed, completely fictitious but typical visitors to Bath.

Mr. Wicksteed, a member of the gentry, has prospered as a result of his investment in the booming sugar plantations in the West Indian colonies. Now, in his mature years, he has come to the spa to take the waters for his gout and to give his young wife and family the chance to enjoy the many pleasures of Bath society.

Many visiting families could only afford to lease one floor of a lodging house. Fellow guests had to share the kitchen and staircase and their servants shared the garetts in the attic. Being well-to-do, Mr Wicksteed has been able to lease a whole house.

On the first floor, we see Mr and Mrs Wicksteed about to leave to promenade the town. These richly ornamented rooms, the "piano nobile", were principally used for entertaining. The second floor, with less decoration and a lower ceiling, was used for bedrooms. Two "Bath Chairmen" have just carried Mr Wicksteed's Uncle Samuel back from the baths and all the way up to his bedroom. He is well wrapped up and, following his physician's advice, will now retire to bed to sweat for an hour.

The children and servants live on the cold and drab attic floor. The children are bored by the pleasures of Bath and Emily, their nurse maid, is having difficulties. They have already thrown their toys into the gutter - which might mean another job for a plumber.

The service quarters in the basement are full of bustle. There were two kitchens, the back one doubling up as the servants' hall and vaults for storing coal, ashes, wood and small beer.

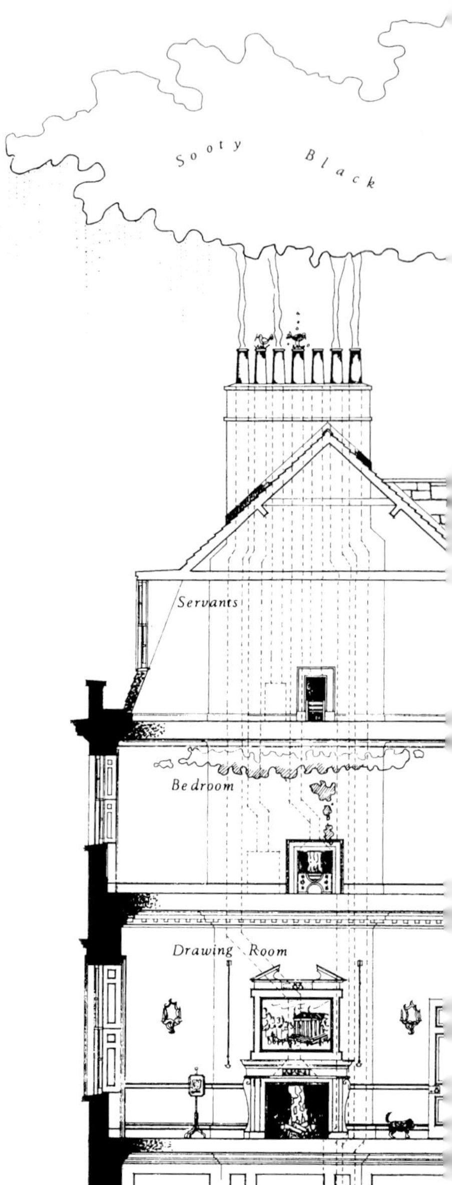

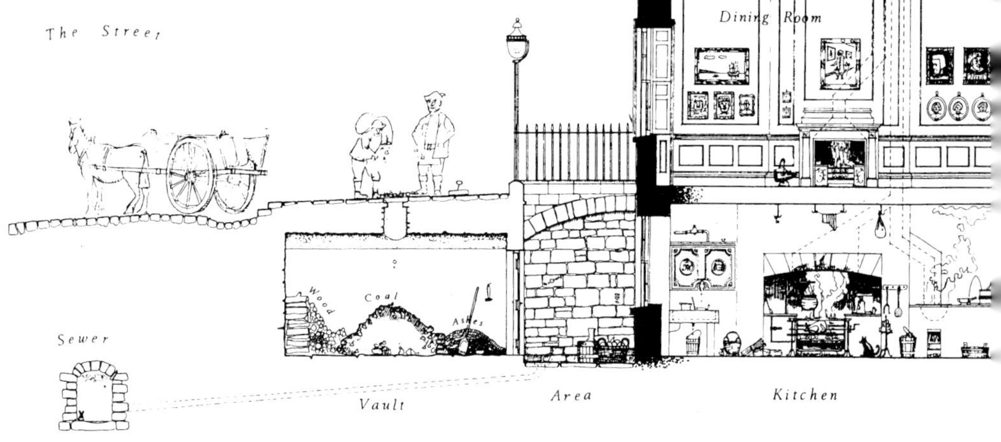

This new house possesses every modern convenience. Fireplaces of this date were designed not to allow smoke into the room but the city itself must have been full of sooty black coal smoke, slowly blackening the new houses. In the evening the rooms would be very gloomy by today's standards, lit by tallow candles which burned poorly and, as they were made from melted animal fat, smelt very unpleasant. The better quality, but expensive, beeswax candles were only used when Mrs Wicksteed was entertaining her new acquaintances.

Unlike most other towns of the period, Bath had a good water supply because of its abundance of springs; this street was supplied by the reservoir in The Circus. Narrow lead pipes called "feathers" tapped into the mains pipes - which were hollowed out elm trunks - and fed a large cistern in the kitchen from which water would be drawn to serve the household.

Flushing water closets for human waste were rare until the early 19th century and a privy in the back garden was used instead. The cesspit below was periodically emptied by "night soil men" who came with their carts in the early hours of the morning. If there was no access at the back, the contents of the cesspit would have to be carried through the house in wooden tubs. Mrs Wicksteed does not deign to descend to the garden and uses the chamber pot in her room, leaving it for her maid Nellie to empty. But - unfortunately for Mrs Wicksteed - Nellie, chamber pot in hand on her way to the privy, has met one of her mistress's admirers in the hall.

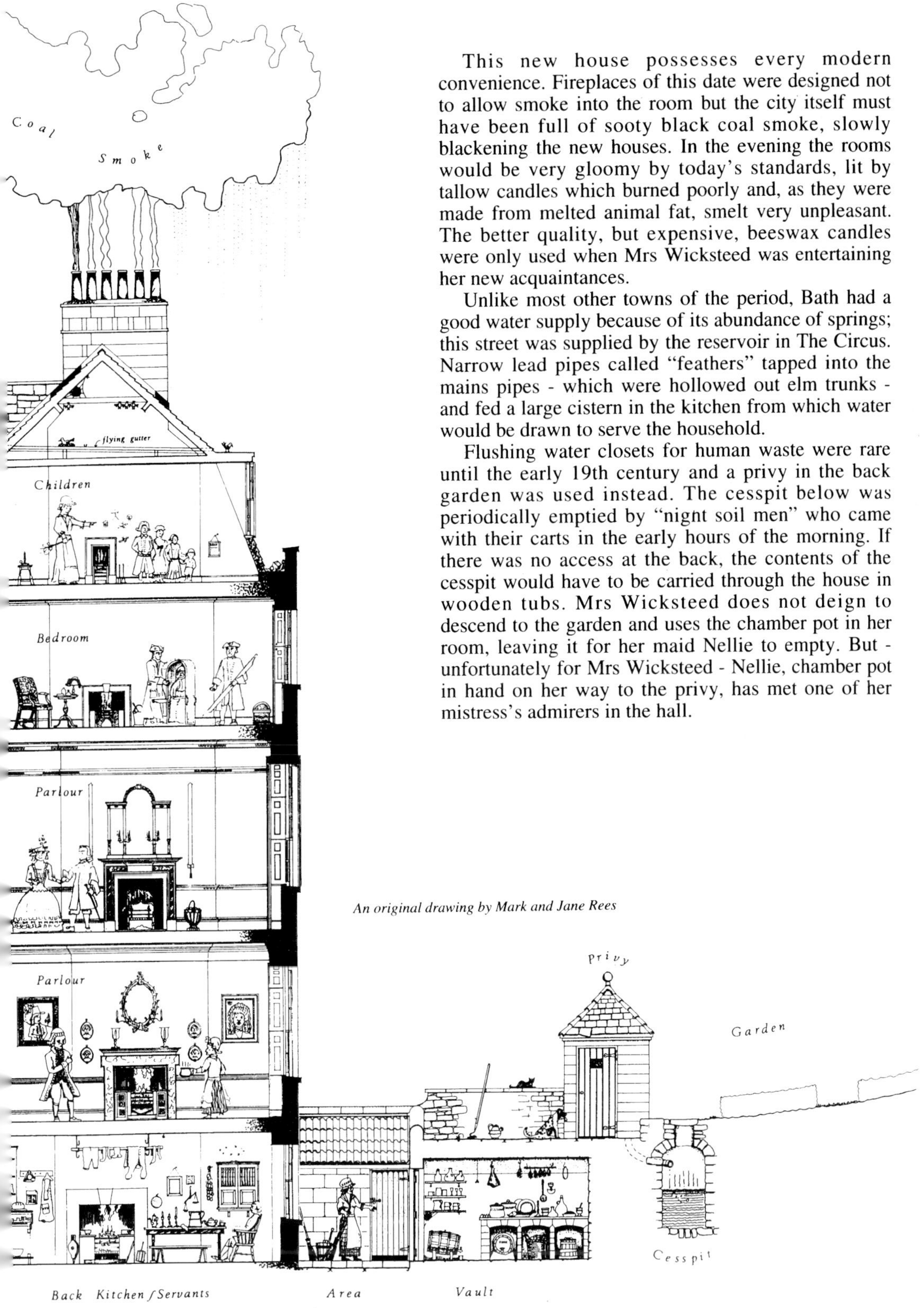

An original drawing by Mark and Jane Rees

Out On The Streets....

Now that the house is furnished and full of life, we have reached the end of the Museum's story. We hope that you will now go out on to the streets of Bath with a fresh insight into the architecture around you.

Many reminders of the bustle and activity of the Georgian city still survive in those streets.

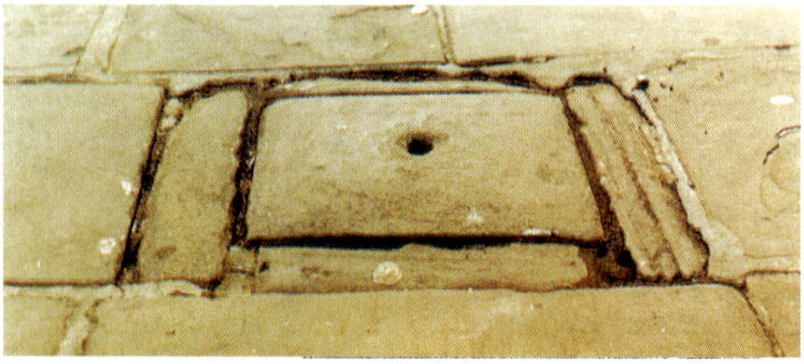

Stone coal hole cover, St Michael's Place
Deliveries of coal were poured down a chute into the cellars under the pavement. Bath is probably the only city where you can see the original removable stone covers to these "coal holes".

"Bath Sun Fire" Insurance Plaque, 3 Queen Square
The Sun Fire Insurance Company was founded in London some years after the Great Fire. It had its own fire service with a branch in Bath. If your house was on fire they would put it out - but only if there was a copper insurance plaque above the door to show that you had paid your subscription.

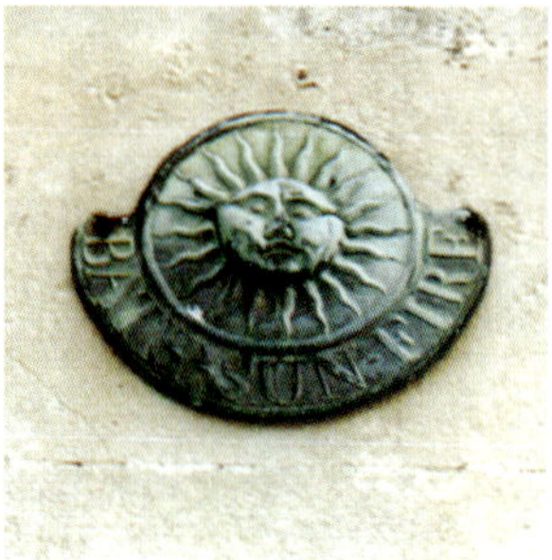

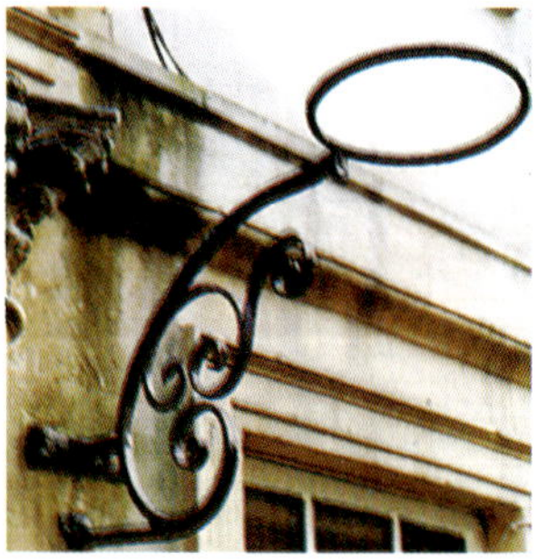

Iron Lamp bracket, North Parade Buildings
The city was dark by night until 1707, when the Corporation ordered every householder to burn candles or lamps outside during the winter months. The rim of the glass globe of this property's oil lamp rested on this iron hoop.

Bell pull at 26 Great Pulteney Street

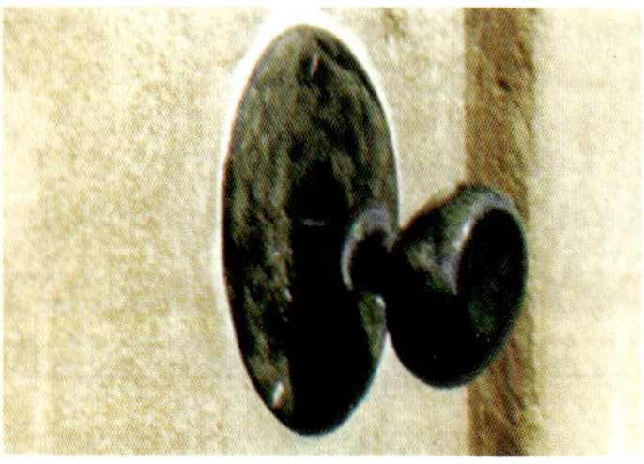

Winch at 14 Alfred Street
Although most goods were supplied to the front door, barrels and other heavy loads were delivered to the basement. This house, like many others, had no steps leading down, so such goods were lowered by a winch.

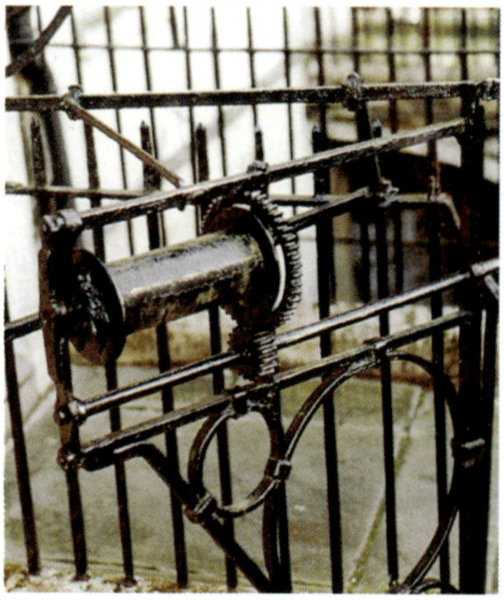

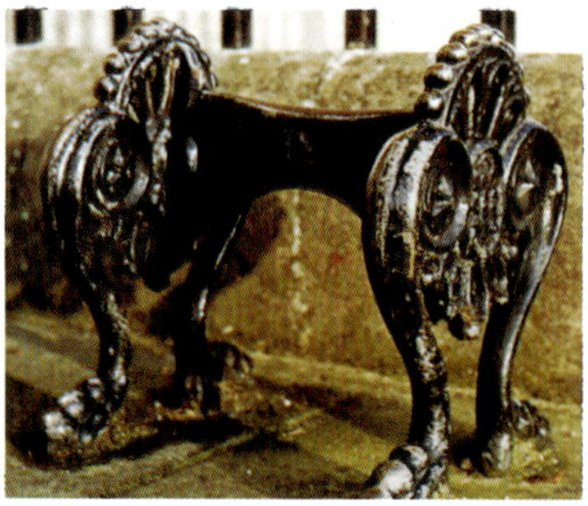

Footscraper at No.1 Royal Crescent

Snuffer at No.1 Royal Crescent
At night your way was lit by flaming torches, carried by "linkboys" or fixed to sedan chairs. This snuffer was for extinguishing the torches when you reached your destination.

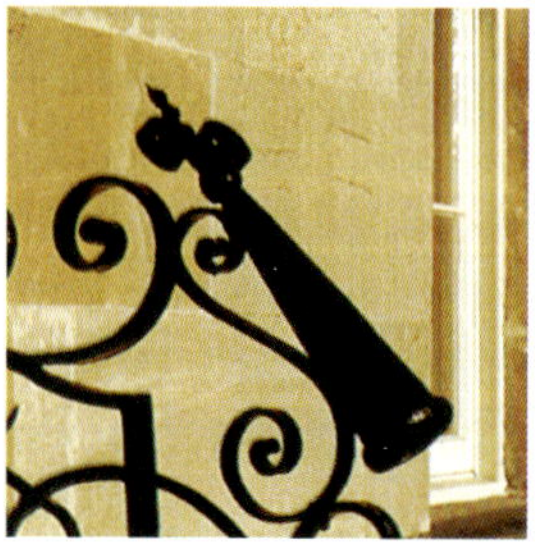

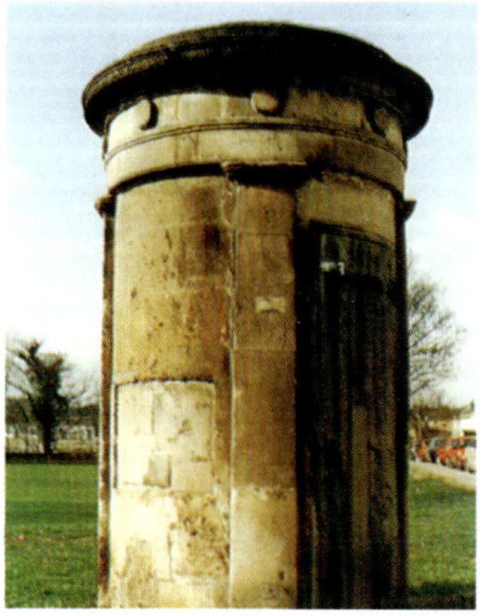

Night watchman's box by Norfolk Crescent.
Before the days of the police force, the parish paid for nightwatchmen known as "beadles" to patrol the streets. One beadle stood guard here, armed, no doubt, with his customary lamp and staff, rattle and watch.